Augustus Mongredien

England's Foreign Policy

An inquiry as to whether we should continue a policy of intervention, or

adopt a policy of isolation

Augustus Mongredien

England's Foreign Policy
*An inquiry as to whether we should continue a policy of intervention, or adopt a
policy of isolation*

ISBN/EAN: 9783337064037

Printed in Europe, USA, Canada, Australia, Japan

Cover: Foto ©Suzi / pixelio.de

More available books at **www.hansebooks.com**

ENGLAND

FOREIGN POLICY;

AN ENQUIRY

AS TO WHETHER WE SHOULD CONTINUE A POLICY
OF INTERVENTION,

OR ADOPT A POLICY OF ISOLATION.

BY

AUGUSTUS MONGREDIEN,

LONDON

EDWARD STANFORD, 6 AND 7 CHARING CROSS.

1871.

PREFACE.

THAT war is a curse to humanity and a foul blot on our boasted civilization, all are agreed. Unless positively indispensable, it is unpardonably criminal.

It is the object of the following pages to show that really necessary wars are of rare occurrence ; and that almost every war which England has waged, owed its origin to mistaken views as to our relations with foreign states.

The subject is one of paramount importance to every adult in the empire, for, if the views here advocated should stand the test of analysis, their adoption as the basis of our future foreign policy will remove evils, from which every member of the community has already suffered much, and may be called upon to suffer more.

It seems probable that public opinion may, at last, be prepared seriously to discuss this vital question, and that the opinions enunciated may find a reflex in the minds of thoughtful men. Recent events have propelled the current of inquiry in that direction, and our leading statesmen show an increasing disposition to concentrate their energies on grave problems at home, instead of wasting them on the affairs of other people abroad.

That good and earnest man, Richard Cobden, with a small but devoted band of adherents, raised, some years ago, the banner of " Peace at any price." Practical men, however, refused their adhesion to a doctrine so extreme. It left no links to connect the engagements to which the past had bound us, with the purely passive course which it enjoined. His theory, carried to its ultimate consequences, provided no defence against unprovoked foreign aggression, and it aimed, generally, at too sudden a conversion of England into Utopia.

Even the more gradual process and more practical methods suggested in these pages for the avoidance of war, may not obtain immediate acceptance, but the writer entertains the firm conviction that the adoption of some such course

is only a question of time. Unless civilization be
mere hypocrisy, we must do more than vehemently
declaim on the wickedness and absurdity of war;
we must earnestly seek, and we shall assuredly
find, the means of dispensing with that savage,
costly, and illogical mode of settling disputes
between rational beings.

The subject is not treated here in a party spirit.
On large questions affecting the honour and welfare of England, the best and ablest men of all
parties have frequently, and of late years, nearly
always, coalesced. They may have differed as
to the means and the minor details, but they
have had the same end in view. The policy here
foreshadowed is of no party, and if it prove to be
based on truth, it commends itself to men of
every shade of political opinion.

The writer pleads guilty beforehand to various
defects in the execution of this work. He ought,
for instance, in order to complete his argument,
to have adduced a larger number of historical
illustrations, and also to have discussed in greater
detail the bearings of our existing treaty-obliga-
tions; but this would have led to the undesirable
result of swelling a small book into a large one;

and of two evils the author has preferred the lesser.

Some repetitions also occur, but they were in-dispensable in grappling with the Protean shapes of fallacies often reappearing in altered verbal forms.

This work puts forth no pretensions to settle the question, but merely aspires to open it up to public discussion.

June, 1871.
HEATHERSIDE,
    BAGSHOT, SURREY.

CONTENTS.

---◆◆◆---

CHAPTER I.

PAGE

Statement of the question 1

CHAPTER II.

How we were drawn into meddling with Continental affairs   2

CHAPTER III.

Necessity for fixed principles in the conduct of our Foreign Policy 3

CHAPTER IV.

What are the advantages, real or supposed, of the old system of mixing ourselves up with European Politics   .   5

CHAPTER V.

First argument adduced in favour of the old policy : "That by interfering in European Politics we may prevent, and ought to prevent, any one of the European States from increasing its territory and power at the expense of another, and thus maintain the 'balance of power.'"   .   6

CHAPTER VI.

Second argument adduced in favour of the old policy : "That unless we identify ourselves with European Politics, and take an active part in arresting the growing ascendancy of some states, and in preserving unimpaired the power of others, we shall run the risk of having to make war under greater disadvantages than we should if the existing distribution of power remained unaltered."   .   11

CHAPTER VII.

PAGE

Third argument adduced in favour of the old policy : "That
we belong to the 'Great European family,' and must
therefore interfere in the family quarrels." 13

CHAPTER VIII.

Fourth argument adduced in favour of the old policy : "That
our retirement from the old policy of interference will be
ascribed to timidity and commercial greed. To timidity,
which compromises our ancient prestige, and reduces us to
the rank of a second-rate or third-rate power ; and to
commercial greed, which enervates a nation, and substitutes
mammon-worship to higher aspirations." 16

CHAPTER IX.

Fifth argument adduced in favour of the old policy : " That,
for instance, unless we interfere to prevent Russia from
conquering the Turks and seizing Constantinople, we
expose our Indian possessions to a formidable attack by
that power." 24

CHAPTER X.

Sixth argument adduced in favour of the old policy : "That
it is inhuman and cowardly to stand by and see one
nation conquered by another ; and that it is our duty to
interfere to prevent it." 27

CHAPTER XI.

Seventh argument adduced in favour of the old policy :
"That interference in European affairs does not necessarily expose us to the danger of war, because we can
interpose our mediation without being compelled to
enforce it by physical force." 35

CHAPTER XII.

PAGE

Eighth argument adduced in favour of the old policy : " That non-interference with European Politics would not preserve us from wars ; as they would or might originate in other sources, such as, 1st. Gratuitous insult or un- provoked attack from foreign states ; 2nd. Outrages on British subjects for which redress was refused ; 3rd. Differences between our own views and those of bel- ligerents as to our duties as neutrals ; 4th. Disputes between our colonies and foreign states, in which we might have to take a part." 42

CHAPTER XIII.

Ninth argument adduced in favour of the old policy : " That without occasional wars the nation might lose its martial prowess and sink into effeminacy ; that we should forfeit our maritime supremacy ; that our naval and military establishments would be so reduced as to court attacks, which we should be powerless to repel." 51

CHAPTER XIV.

Tenth argument adduced in favour of the old policy : " That old alliances and existing treaties to which we are still bound prevent the adoption of the policy of isolation advocated in this essay." 63

CHAPTER XV.

Search after more arguments adducible in favour of the old policy 68

CHAPTER XVI.

The general advantages of a policy of isolation 71

CHAPTER XVII.

First argument in favour of the policy of isolation : " Avoid- ance of unnecessary wars." 76

CHAPTER XVIII.

PAGE

Second argument in favour of the policy ot isolation : " Removal of the inconveniences attending—1st. A large standing army. 2nd. Costly warlike preparations. 3rd. The suspension of internal improvements on account of external political complications." 79

CHAPTER XIX.

Third argument in favour of the policy of isolation : " The cessation of jealousy and distrust on the part of foreign states." 82

CHAPTER XX.

Fourth argument in favour of the policy of isolation : " It would conduce to and facilitate the settlement of international disputes by arbitration." 84

CHAPTER XXI.

Fifth argument in favour of the policy of isolation : " Our example may induce other states to adopt a similar policy." 90

CHAPTER XXII.

Europe not a confederation of states. Tendency of communities to consolidate into lingual groups 92

CHAPTER XXIII.

Influence of war on the interests of wage-receivers . . . 97

CHAPTER XXIV.

Movement of political power and intellectual energy from East to West 102

CHAPTER XXV.

Presumptive vast increase of the population of the globe, and as to the races of which this increase will be mostly composed. Probable preponderance of the Anglo-Saxon race 108

ENGLAND'S FOREIGN POLICY.

CHAPTER I.

Statement of the question.

OUGHT the destiny of England to be permanently bound up with that of Continental Europe? or—

Ought England to free herself from the trammels of the European political system, and to pursue an independent and self-dependent career?

To put the question in other terms :—

Is it right and expedient for England to regulate, or to attempt to regulate the distribution of power and of territory amongst the various European States? or—

Is it right and expedient for England to confine her attention to her own concerns, and adopt a policy of isolation?

This is truly an important issue, worthy of free and fearless discussion.

The one is the policy which, sometimes vigorously and consistently, sometimes feebly and hesitatingly, has hitherto been followed by our statesmen.

The other is the policy advocated in the following pages.

———◆——

CHAPTER II.

How we were drawn into meddling with Continental affairs.

IN 1066 the Duke of Normandy made himself King of England ; hence our first fatal possession of territorial and political interests on the continent of Europe. The disastrous wars which their preservation required decimated England during five centuries, and the loss of Calais, under Mary, fittingly closed the sanguinary drama. But our importation of King William III., and our identification with his crusade against Louis XIV., again drew us into the vortex of European politics, from which we had scarcely been extricated by Mrs. Masham's peace with France, when another imported king, George I., brought with him the incumbrance of Hanover. The preservation of that dreary province became a leading feature of our state policy, and involved us in fresh wars and fresh complications with European states. Finally, the old delusive notion adopted by Pitt, and handed traditionally down to Palmerston, that we both could and should maintain the "balance of power" in Europe, brings us down to the present era, in which men are beginning to question the truth of that doctrine, and to deplore the terrible calamities it has occasioned.

It is owing to these extrinsic circumstances that we have never availed ourselves of all the advantages afforded us by our insular position.

CHAPTER III.

Necessity for fixed principles in the conduct of our foreign policy.

IN respect to questions concerning internal reforms or domestic improvements, there is ample time for opinions to mature; and delay, whilst it may postpone progress, does not cause disaster. It is otherwise with questions of foreign policy. The emergencies on which it has to pronounce are frequently sudden and unexpected, and have to be met with prompti-

tude and decision. A wavering policy—a trust
to the shifting sands of expediency—a recourse
to wordy mediation, which implies the pale
shadow, but not the reality, of a threat—all
these are the devices of a weak government,
and are, with contemptuous courtesy, jostled
aside by earnest men bent on vigorous action.

To will weakly is a vital error in the conduct
of political affairs.   We drifted into the Crimean
War by "willing weakly." We overcame the
Indian insurrection by willing strongly.   In
order to go straight to an object, we must keep
it clearly in sight.   If we decide on the policy
of intervention, with all its positive evils and its
few nugatory advantages, we ought to pursue it
thoroughly, and act on it with boldness and
decision.   It is true that we shall not avoid
wars, occasional defeats, treachery of allies, and
general disappointment at results ; but we shall
at least save our honour and preserve our
dignity, which we compromise by professing a
policy which we are reluctant to carry out, and
by aspiring to a position which we are un-
prepared to maintain by force of arms.*

* A writer in the ' Quarterly Review ' (January, 1871, p. 282)
remarks strongly on "the indecision and half-heartedness which,
n foreign policy, condemns us to a part which is the ideal
neither of the old English nor of the new Manchester school—
which is neither dignified nor cheap," &c.

If, on the other hand, we decide on a policy of non-intervention, we must take care that it be so in reality and not merely in name. The principle should be clearly recognised and openly proclaimed, so as to leave no ambiguity as to our course under any given circumstances, however suddenly they may arise.

Whichever system be adopted, let us have fixed principles and a decided policy.

------·------

CHAPTER IV.

What are the advantages, real or supposed, of the old system of mixing ourselves up with European politics.

An attempt will here be made to collect every argument bearing on the subject, and to examine each fairly, but fearlessly ; with severe analysis, but with no less severe impartiality. Much of what is contained in the following chapters has been already said or written by various persons at various times ; and to that sagacious thinker, Richard Cobden, is due the merit of having first brought the question prominently before the public. He then had but few listeners, whilst in the present day the community are, of their own accord, turning their thoughts in that direction, and the public mind seems ripe for a thorough consideration and discussion of the subject.

———•———

CHAPTER V.

First argument adduced in favour of the old policy.

THAT BY INTERFERING IN EUROPEAN POLITICS WE MAY PREVENT, AND OUGHT TO PREVENT, ANY ONE OF THE EUROPEAN STATES FROM INCREASING ITS TERRI- TORY AND POWER AT THE EXPENSE OF ANOTHER, AND THUS MAINTAIN THE "BALANCE OF POWER."

To analyse this argument thoroughly we must inquire—

What is the real meaning of the words " balance of power?"

Whether it is right to maintain it?

Whether it is expedient to maintain it?

Whether it is possible to maintain it?

To maintain the balance of power simply means to preserve (by force of arms, if neces- sary) the exact relative positions of the Euro- pean states actually existing at the time. It by no means implies the equalization of power. It leaves the strong states still strong, and the weak states still weak, and only interdicts change from the *status quo* of each state.

Supposing this doctrine of the necessity for the forcible repression of territorial change to be true in principle and possible in practice, and supposing its successful application two, three, or four centuries ago, what would now be the condition of Europe?

The balance of power in 1570 would have implied the supremacy of Spain—the forcible repression of religious as well as of political change—and its successful maintenance by physical force would have arrested all progress, and perpetuated a state of things which no one can now contemplate as desirable.

But if the doctrine of maintenance of the balance of power be true in 1870, it must surely have been true in 1570. The same reasons that can be quoted in its favour now, were equally fitting then. Unless, indeed, it may be contended that in 1570 European institutions were imperfect and required change, whereas in 1870 we have reached the point from which any further alteration would be unwise. Can such a proposition be advanced?

It would not be *right* to maintain the balance of power, even had we the ability, because by so doing we assume that all change

C

in the distribution of power must be for evil—an assumption which implies a knowledge of the future which we do not possess, and a distrust of innovation which history does not warrant.

Leaving the question of abstract right, which has very little weight in the conduct of political affairs, let us look at the *expediency* of maintaining the balance of power; that is, of opposing changes in the existing relative position of one European state to another. This expediency depends on the value of the object attained as compared with the cost of attaining it. Viewed in this light, its expediency vanishes at once, and its utter inexpediency becomes clearly visible. In all the wars we have waged to maintain this chimera, "the balance of power," we find a minimum of benefit to set off against hundreds of thousands of lives and hundreds of millions of debt.

The war waged against Louis XIV. to maintain the balance of power, supposed to be infringed by his grandson's occupation of the Spanish throne, lasted many years, inflicted infinite misery on the French people, cost us and them torrents of blood, burthened us with our first national debt (doubtfully compensated by the glories of Ramilies and Blenheim); and what was the result? We gained no object whatever, and the Bourbons remained in possession of the throne of Spain.

The twenty years' war with France, which terminated in 1815, was equally barren in results to us, and infinitely more costly.

Can it be expedient to pursue a policy which, on the one hand implies death and poverty to countless thousands ; and on the other is productive of no other benefit than the very distant chance that such a policy might possibly prevent a state of things which may, or may not, at some remote period, savour of danger to our posterity ?

But, even supposing the *right* and the *expediency* of preventing changes in the distribution of power throughout Europe, is it *possible* for us to accomplish that object ?

History, which impartially chronicles the real results of political experiments, teaches us that in small matters, and temporarily, we may have partially succeeded ; but that as regards large and important changes, we have either shrunk from taking any action, or have failed in averting them. What was Prussia a century ago, and what is she now ? What was Poland in the time of Sobieski, and what is she now ? What was Italy at the beginning of this century, and what is she now ? The important revolutions which have taken place in the destinies of these three nations have changed the face of Europe, and shifted the pivot on which the "balance of power" was permanently to have revolved. What part have we taken in preventing or producing them? The fact is that these great changes took place without any reference whatever to the assumption on our part that we are arbiters of the limits with which each state is to be contented; and our passive submission to the new "balance of power" which these events created is a sufficient acknowledgment that it was beyond our power to maintain the old one.

In short, all human barriers to the law of progress are futilities, and in spite of the unnatural interference of physical force to keep things stationary and arrest the irresistible course of events, human destiny still moves on *in omne volubilis ævum.*

CHAPTER VI.

Second argument adduced in favour of the old policy.

THAT UNLESS WE IDENTIFY OURSELVES WITH EURO-
PEAN POLITICS, AND TAKE AN ACTIVE PART IN AR-
RESTING THE GROWING ASCENDANCY OF SOME STATES,
AND IN PRESERVING UNIMPAIRED THE POWER OF
OTHERS, WE SHALL RUN THE RISK OF HAVING TO
MAKE WAR UNDER GREATER DISADVANTAGES THAN
WE SHOULD IF THE EXISTING DISTRIBUTION OF POWER
REMAINED UNALTERED.

THIS argument presupposes—

1st. That a state which increases its territorial
possessions at the expense of its neighbours
becomes thereby a more formidable enemy than
before.

2nd. That a state having so increased its
territory would, from that circumstance, derive
peculiar incentives to attack us.

3rd. That with a view of avoiding the possible
contingency of such future attack, it is good
policy to assume a hostile attitude towards such
a state, even if it should lead to immediate war.

As to the first point, history teaches us that
conquest weakens the conqueror. Triumphs
which result in territorial acquisitions may en-
twine laurels round the brow of the victor, but

they undermine his real power. The subjugator
of alien nationalities spreads a thorny bed for
his successors, if not, as in many instances, for
himself. A large empire built up by force of
arms, out of heterogeneous materials, contains
in its very composition the seeds of decay.
" *Mole ruit suâ.*" The conquered nations have
always proved thorns in the sides of their conquerors. The fall of Spain from her "high
estate" was in no small degree the result of her
impotent efforts to retain her hold over Holland
and Naples. Poland is even now a source of
weakness, not of strength, to Russia. Napoleon's
conquests shed a delusive lustre over his short-
lived career, but they proved his ruin and caused
his downfall. Thus we may fairly argue that
a state which has by conquest absorbed another
nation does *not* thereby become a more formidable enemy.

A state that stood in such a position would
have many motives for courting our friendship,
none for provoking our enmity. Encumbered
by its very aggrandizement,—presenting a wider
surface for attack whilst weakened by internal
disquietude,—requiring its strength for repres-
sive action at home, and having none to spare
for aggressive action abroad—such a state would
certainly be less disposed to assail, and more

powerless to harm, than before it was enfeebled by extension.

Under the circumstances referred to above, to risk an immediate war in order to avert the mere contingency of a war at some future period, cannot be deemed a wise policy. It is very much akin to the act of a man who commits suicide to avoid going into battle. It is founded, not on real courage, but on a fidgety and pusillanimous distrust of the future. So panics originate disasters which, but for them, might never have occurred, and thus vague and sickly apprehensions of evil have on many occasions actually brought it about.

CHAPTER VII.

Third argument adduced in favour of the old policy.

THAT WE BELONG TO THE "GREAT EUROPEAN FAMILY," AND MUST THEREFORE INTERFERE IN THE FAMILY QUARRELS.

THIS proposition is based on an unmeaning phrase, the substance of which, tested by analysis, vanishes into thin air. There is no such thing as the "European family" in the sense in which the words are generally used. Europe, by far the smallest quarter of the globe, is mapped out into a certain number of independent states, each with its own distinct government (good or bad), and each with its own separate interests and policy, properly or improperly understood. Every state fears, mistrusts, and, more or less, hates the others, from a foolish belief that has hitherto prevailed that their respective interests are antagonistic, and that if one state becomes too prosperous and powerful, it must be "put down," or the rest will forfeit their own power and prosperity.

These states no more constitute an " European family," than the inmates of the different houses in Baker Street constitute a " Baker Street family." No doubt, proximity necessitates relations of some kind. Families residing in neighbouring houses may form book-clubs, or combine to remove some common nuisance at common expense. So governments, for mutual convenience, must enter into conventions for postal arrangements, the extradition of criminals, &c.

But supposing that Smith of No. 499 Baker Street has a quarrel or a law-suit with Jones of No. 501, does Robinson of No. 500 dream of interfering, merely because they all belong to the " Baker Street family ?"

Similarly, if one European state embarks in a war against another, there are certainly no "family ties" by which we are bound to increase the carnage by taking an active part in such war. There may, or may not, be other reasons for our so doing; but the supposed fact of our belonging to the "great European family," which has no existence, is evidently no reason at all.

If we are under any family obligations whatever, it could only be towards the great Anglo-Saxon race which is now gradually overspreading the globe. Its members are our own kith and kin, they are descended from a common ancestry, speak our own language, imbue their minds with the same poetry and literature, and inherit the same tastes and feelings. But as to the Teutonic, Celtic, Latin, Sclavonic, Scandinavian, and other races, large and small, peopling Europe, whilst we may and should preserve towards them the most friendly attitude, there are no "family ties" which can morally compel us to share their fortunes or misfortunes.

And so we now dismiss the euphonious but delusive phrase, "great European family," as a mere rhetorical flourish.

CHAPTER VIII.

Fourth argument adduced in favour of the old policy.

THAT OUR RETIREMENT FROM THE OLD POLICY OF INTERFERENCE WILL BE ASCRIBED TO TIMIDITY AND COMMERCIAL GREED. TO TIMIDITY,—WHICH COMPROMISES OUR ANCIENT PRESTIGE, AND REDUCES US TO THE RANK OF A SECOND-RATE OR THIRD-RATE POWER ; AND TO COMMERCIAL GREED,—WHICH ENERVATES A NATION, AND SUBSTITUTES MAMMON-WORSHIP FOR HIGHER ASPIRATIONS.

THIS fallacy is based on the following two assumptions :—

1st. That our *prestige*, and our claim to rank as a first-rate power, are, in great measure, dependent on the influence we may exercise over the affairs of other states.

2nd. That the extension of our commerce is a secondary object as compared with the maintenance of our political influence.

Both assumptions are essentially erroneous and fatally misleading, as may, we think, be easily demonstrated.

The rank which we, as a state, may occupy in the estimation of other nations is, substantially, a matter of no importance to us, provided our people be prosperous and happy. *Felicitas populi*

suprema lex. The final cause of all government
is the welfare of the community. Till that is
fully realized, all hankering after glory and
" prestige " is misplaced. Many think it patriotic
(is it more than snobbish ?) to scheme how to
make the English nation appear " big,"—to frame
cunning devices to induce foreigners to believe
us more powerful than we are—to boast of the
high rank we occupy in the scale of nations. But
these pretensions are a sham and an imposture
if not supported by the possession of real power.
It is no substitute for it to make a scenic display
of fussy interference in other nation's affairs.
Our prestige, if it be of any importance to preserve
it, must ultimately depend exclusively on our
actual might ; and no brandishing of two-handed
swords, or pretentious display of wooden artillery,
will long succeed in maintaining the deception.

But we do possess the requisite power to hold
our high position, and that power will continue
to increase and accumulate as long as it remains
unwasted by war. There could therefore be no
more opportune moment for announcing that our
future foreign policy (with such exceptions as
existing treaties may exact, as long as they
remain in force) shall be abstinence of intervention
in all quarrels to which we are not direct parties,
abstention from alliances with other states, a

policy of friendship with all, partnership with none—that it shall be, in short, a policy of isolation. Such a policy, distinctly proclaimed, might indeed at first startle Europe, and doubts might be expressed, if not really felt, as to our inflexible adherence to it ; but most certainly it would afford no pretext for any serious imputation of either timidity or weakness.

On the other hand, such imputation of timidity and weakness is quite justified under our present system of diplomacy, because our interference with European politics is occasional, fitful, and vacillating. Amidst the complicated relations with foreign states in which the system hitherto pursued has involved us, our continental neighbours cannot understand how it is, that, like men in a tertian ague, we should have our hot and cold fits of intermeddling. Under one ministry we rush headlong into the European fray ; whilst under another, we hesitate, parley, and, " willing to wound, and yet afraid to strike," resort to every plausible expedient to evade our engagements either positive or implied.

In the first case, we sacrifice blood and treasure for the accomplishment of some object which, in some instances, we fail in accomplishing (which is the most frequent result) ; or which, in others, having accomplished for the time, we shall have to reaccomplish before many years elapse; or which, even, in case of success, is not worth the thousandth part of what we have sacrificed for its accomplishment.

In the second case, that of the vacillating policy (which proclaims our right and recognizes our liability to interfere with the broils of the "great European family," whilst resorting to all manner of shifts and expedients to shuffle out of the feud)—it places us in a false position, and makes it quite natural that foreigners should ascribe, or affect to ascribe, such manœuvres to timidity or conscious weakness.

Far from admitting that the extension of commerce is secondary in importance to the maintenance of political influence, we assert—

1st. That the extension of commerce is an immense and unmixed benefit to all mankind, and as such, of quite primary importance. It is the interchange of one nation's superfluities for another nation's superfluities, both being converted into blessings by the transfer. It is the foremost advantage, as it is the highest aim of the social system. Government itself is only instituted to facilitate human intercourse on principles of justice, by repressing violence and fraud.

2nd. That the extension of political influence

is a childish bauble, born of self-conceit, and
conducing to international jealousy, intrigues,
and animosities, and frequently culminating in
useless war with all its horrors.

If this be so, why should we blush to avow, or
rather why should we not glory in avowing, that
one of our objects in seeking to remain at peace
with all men is to promote the general extension
of commerce in its widest and most cosmopolitan
sense ?

Commerce is the only game at which both
players win.   Interchange is   spontaneous.
Buyers prize sellers' goods beyond what they
pay for them, sellers prize buyers' money beyond
what they give for it.   Both parties are satisfied
and benefited.

Happy would it be for the world at large, if
the peaceful interchange between one country
and another, of those things which are physically
useful and   morally beneficial to   each, were
acknowledged to be the main object, and indeed,
the final cause of civilization !

Commerce is all this.   It includes the production of the raw materials which the bounteous
earth yields us at our bidding (agriculture,
mining, &c.) ;   the fabrication of those raw
materials into articles of utility and comfort
(manufactures, architecture, &c.) ;   the production

of whatever ministers to the æsthetic element of our nature, whether in the shape of new scientific truths, or of novel contrasts and parallels between the past and the present, or of freshly detected and fittingly expressed harmonies between our spiritual being and external nature (science, literature, poetry, and the fine arts) ; and finally, it includes the distribution of all the valuable objects so produced, amongst the denizens of different countries in conformity with the laws of demand and supply.*

* That the discoveries of science, the political deductions of historians, the tentative theories of philosophers, the creations of poetry, and the artistic productions of musicians, painters, and sculptors, should come under the category of "commerce," will be considered a novel, but is not the less a perfectly accurate, classification. All these processes imply the production of something valuable to the world at large, for which a certain price is paid by the community, in the shape of either copyright to authors, or purchase-money to painters and sculptors. This price varies according to the estimation (not unfrequently erroneous) in which the results of such labours are held by the public ; and they are thus subject to the commercial law of supply and demand. Their marketable value entirely depends on competition. When the wave of national prosperity rolls high, great prices are paid. When a period of financial embarrassment supervenes, the demand slackens, the poets and painters suffer from the "dulness of the market," and have to submit to lower prices for their commodities. The vicissitudes of value which their performances undergo are identical with those experienced by the operations of the weaver or miner. Until an adequate fund (generally called capital) be formed by the surplus of production over consumption (in other words, by savings), literature, science, and art cannot exist, and their votaries are

Such is the noble and humanizing mission of commerce; and yet, in this boasted era of progress we are still under the dominion of the same prejudices which, in dark and barbarous ages, condemned commercial pursuits to comparative ignominy, and exalted military violence and priestly craft to the places of honour.

Even now, the claims of commerce to respect are reluctantly admitted, and a mercantile is considered as less honourable than what is called a professional career. We think that careful inquiry leads us to an opposite conclusion.

Commerce effects a *positive* good by the production and distribution of those things that conduce to man's well-being.

Professional pursuits can, at best, only aim at a *negative* good, by neutralizing the evils which result from our vices and imperfections. They may be necessary, but their necessity is based on the weakness or wickedness of man. They contribute nothing to our enjoyments, but do something towards mitigating our afflictions. The vocation of soldiers, statesmen, lawyers, clergymen, physicians, &c., is to repel invasion, curb turbulence, repress evildoers, counteract

---

entirely dependent on material wealth for the resources which enable them to devote themselves to their elevating pursuits.

injustice, restrain immorality, heal disease, &c. &c., and generally to prevent, remedy, or punish the calamities and misdeeds springing from the imperfections of our nature. These tasks are useful, nay, indispensable ; and so are many offices of an ignoble sort which necessity requires that some members of the community should perform ; but they do not confer on the functionaries any patent of superiority over the producers of the very wealth out of which their salaries are paid.

Away then with the senseless notion that it is inglorious to shun unnecessary (and therefore atrociously wicked) wars in order to devote ourselves to commerce with its wide-spread blessings!

As to the "substitution of Mammon-worship for higher aspirations," it is a mere figure of speech. If devotion to industry and to the arts of peace be "Mammon-worship," and if war and carnage be the "higher aspirations," then we uphold the "substitution." If the phrase does not convey that meaning, it conveys none ; and so we dismiss it.

———◆———

D

CHAPTER IX.

Fifth argument adduced in favour of the old policy.

THAT, FOR INSTANCE, UNLESS WE INTERFERE TO PREVENT RUSSIA FROM CONQUERING THE TURKS AND SEIZING CONSTANTINOPLE, WE EXPOSE OUR INDIAN POSSESSIONS TO A FORMIDABLE ATTACK BY THAT POWER.

THE abstract question of right or wrong is here abandoned, and the argument "ad Angliam" ingenuously resorted to. Let us analyze it.

Is it by any means certain that, unless we interfere, Russia will succeed in the designs which she is accused of entertaining on Constantinople? Many other difficulties besides those which we might interpose would cross her path; and such checks would have the advantage of being local, natural, and permanent, and more constant and effectual in their operation than the fitful and arbitrary antagonism of a state so distant as we are from the scene of conflict. We deny the implied assumption that, if England were neutral, Constantinople would assuredly become Russian property.

But let us admit a proposition so flattering to our self-love as that England is the only barrier to Russian aggrandizement, and then let us inquire how many wars (we mean homicidal wars, for the diplomatic hostilities are unremitting) are we to wage to keep Constantinople out of Russian clutches? *Usque quo tandem?* How long is the struggle to continue? If the argument to which this is a reply be well-founded, we must look for repetitions of Crimean campaigns every time that Russia casts a leer of concupiscence towards Turkey. This implies at least one war to each generation, or, say, three wars per century. A mighty cost indeed! And for what purpose? To obviate the very remote contingency of having, at some future indefinite period, to defend our Indian possessions from Russian attack. This policy involves the necessity of waging war with Russia at periodical intervals on or near her own territory, in order to avoid the barely possible chance of collision with that state at some distant time in a distant part of Asia. Is this wisdom, or is it folly?

Whoever will take a map, and examine how very little nearer to India Russia would be brought by the possession of Constantinople, will understand how groundless a panic has involved us in the labyrinthine mazes of the " Eastern question." By land, the distance would be just as great as before. By sea, now that Russia is allowed to build fleets in the Black Sea, the difference between launching them from Sevastopol or from Constantinople is infinitesimal. It is unreasonable that for such a trifle we should be called upon to shed the blood of our brethren, to spend the money wrung from the earnings of our producers, and arrest the course of our national prosperity.

But even admitting that Russia should succeed in occupying Constantinople, it is very questionable if she could long maintain her hold. A popular delusion erroneously assumes that the Greek and other Christian populations which practically constitute Turkey entertain Russian sympathies. Quite the contrary. They fear and distrust the Muscovite. That fear and distrust pale, it is true, before the hatred and contempt they nourish for the Turk. But they keep an eye on Constantinople for themselves, as the metropolis of a future Byzantine empire, and would not quietly submit to a substitution of Russian for Turkish domination.

Moreover, the Russian empire is already too extensive. Fresh conquests over alien nationalities, with a different language, dissimilar habits, and antagonistic views and aspirations, would be elements of weakness, not of strength.

As for the Turks, they are a poor, effete, worn-out race, who are only "encamped in Europe," who exist on sufferance, who are utterly incapable of progress, and whom we have hitherto patronized, certainly not for their intrinsic merits, but merely as political stop-gaps, for purposes at once selfish and mistaken.

———•———

CHAPTER X.

Sixth argument adduced in favour of the old policy.

THAT IT IS INHUMAN AND COWARDLY TO STAND BY AND SEE ONE NATION CONQUERED BY ANOTHER ; AND THAT IT IS OUR DUTY TO INTERFERE TO PREVENT IT.

THIS argument shunts the question of right or wrong on to the question of strength or weakness. It implies that we are to side, not with the party whose quarrel is just, but with the party that may happen to be defeated. If a wrongful aggressor meet with discomfiture (and this may sometimes occur), it is proposed that we should side with him, not because he is right, but because he is vanquished. But as we cannot, when the war breaks out, foretell its issue, the proposed policy implies that we must remain passive until one of the belligerents is overthrown, and then, regardless of the justice or injustice of his cause, sacrifice our blood and treasure in an attempt to retrieve his fortunes. Truly a daring paradox! But as it is a rather popular one, it is entitled to thorough examination.

If forcible interference in the quarrels between two or more foreign states could ever be justifiable, it must take place at the outset of the quarrel, when, the grounds of dispute being duly sifted, the interfering state ought naturally to espouse the cause which it deems right and just. Any other assumption implies hostility to right and alliance with injustice, and would no longer be intervention in the sense of equitable mediation, but intervention in the sense of blind partisanship. The most determined advocate of interference would hardly profess on the eve of the conflict to interfere on behalf of the party that was in the wrong. It would read thus:— "You, B, are in the right, but unless you yield to A's unjust demands, we shall make common cause with A, and compel you, by force of arms, to give way."

But if we interpose on behalf of the side whose quarrel appears to us just, and if that side should prove victorious—what then? Are we sure that our victorious ally will be moderate in his triumph, and not seek to reap the utmost material advantages in his power? In the latter case, instead of merely "standing by" and seeing one nation conquered by another, we should actually become *participes criminis*, and be accomplices in the very result which it is alleged that it is "inhuman and cowardly" not to prevent by forcible interference. The only way to repair so "untoward an event," would be for us to change sides when the tide of fortune flowed too rapidly in favour of our allies and ourselves, and, veering suddenly round, join our adversaries, undo our work, and shed more blood and spend more treasure in trying to turn the tide of victory in favour of our late antagonists. We should thus enjoy the glory and bear the suffering of two wars instead of one. In return we may or may not have preserved (for a time) the "balance of power," and shall certainly have reaped the ill-will of both sides.

The dilemma just described may, however, be avoided if, ignoring all consideration of which of the two parties about to engage in hostilities is in the right or which is in the wrong, we simply wait to see which is victorious, and then try to redress the balance by interfering, forcibly if necessary, in favour of the vanquished party.

This chivalrous, not to say Quixotic, course is, however, open to many objections.

1st. If our assistance should turn the scale, and the vanquished became the victorious party, we may have transferred the victory to the side that was originally in the wrong. If so, we shall have helped to enforce compliance with unreasonable demands, and become accessories to the perpetration of an injustice.

2nd. At all events, by identifying ourselves with the losing side, we undertake the very arduous task of arresting the triumphant course of the conqueror, and subduing an enemy flushed with success, and fully organised for, as well as inured to, warlike operations. No doubt there is a spice of romance in the adoption of such a course. " *Victrix causa Diis placuit, sed victa Catoni.*" But what can be said as to its prudence? It would necessitate on our part most vigorous efforts and unsparing sacrifices. Not a household in the country but would have to lament some loss or submit to some privation. In case of success (so dearly purchased), we but add a fresh link to the chain which connects us with the vicissitudes of European states. In case of failure, we have, at a heavy cost, exhibited our impotency. The conquerors remain conquerors in spite of our aid to the conquered, and the position of the latter is made worse by that very circumstance. As long as we remained neutral our peaceful mediation might have proved of some avail. But an abortive attempt at forcible interference would not only deprive us of all influence as inter-cessors, but embitter the hostility of the victors, by prolonging the resistance of their opponents.

It was during the eighteenth century that the "balance of power" became the acknowledged idol of politicians, and the doctrine of interven-tion commanded universal assent. Nevertheless, during that period many important changes took place in the distribution of European territory, with several of which our ancestors did not even seek to interfere. For instance, they were "inhuman and cowardly" enough to stand by and witness, with no more than a faint protest, the partition of Poland, the cession of Silesia to Prussia, and the absorption by Russia of Fin-land. If in the palmy days of the intervention system its staunchest adherents allowed such flagrant violations of the "balance of power" to pass unnoticed, this apparent indifference arose no doubt from the evident futility of any forcible attempt to prevent them, and not, as the argument we are canvassing presupposes, from inhumanity or cowardice.

Undoubtedly, if we could, by our "good offices," and by appealing to the victors on the various pleas of humanity — of the voice of public opinion—and of their own ulterior interests—promote a peaceful and honourable solution of the difficulty, it is clearly our bounden duty to use our utmost efforts towards that end.   Indeed, no war ever occurs in which such endeavours to either prevent its outbreak or shorten its duration have not been made by one or more of the neutral powers.

There can be no difference of opinion as to the moral obligation of every government to resort to every peaceful expedient to maintain or to restore peace.   Unfortunately this style of intervention is seldom successful until both belligerents are fairly exhausted by, and weary of, the struggle.   Whilst the contending parties are under the dominion of mutual hatred and scorn —whilst the animal passions rage uncontrolled, —ere the hot blood has had time to cool—what chance has the " still small voice" of reason and humanity of being listened to ?

And yet if the object in view be to prevent or suspend the effusion of blood, it can only be accomplished by pacific intercession.   For the moment interference steps beyond the bounds of moral suasion and assumes the shape of a threat, the interfering state becomes involved in the war. It coalesces with one side or the other, and from the condition of a neutral sinks into that of a belligerent; "*Desinit in piscem mulier formosa supernè.*" The consequence is, that not only the effusion of blood is unarrested, but that it flows in a still wider stream. But the evil does not stop here. Whenever one neutral state is drawn into the vortex of hostilities, others are nearly sure to follow, some on one side, some on the other, until the conflagration becomes general, and the efforts professedly made to put an end to the carnage have only served to increase it indefinitely, by prolonging the duration, and enlarging the area of the war.

It is quite an open question whether a nation that is undergoing defeat be really benefited by armed intervention on her behalf. Few nations are permanently conquered. They may be prostrated, but they seldom remain prostrate. It is better for their own dignity and self-respect that they should rise again by their own efforts, than that they should have the period of their rise hastened by foreign intervention. In the latter case there arises an uneasy sense of self-insufficiency which seeks relief in an exaggerated self-assertion, bearing a strong resemblance to ingratitude towards the state which afforded such assistance. Indeed, who can say how much, after all, such assistance did contribute towards effecting relief? Spain was overrun by Napoleon's armies, and, for a time, was ruled by a puppet-king of his appointing. Assisted by England, she eventually threw off the yoke —but was it Wellington, or was it Moscow, that achieved her liberation? Napoleon's defeats in 1813 would have enabled Spain to free herself without foreign aid. On the other hand, had Napoleon's victorious career been unchecked, is it by any means certain that the assistance of England would have ultimately saved Spain from French domination? It is quite open to Spain to suggest that, in the first case, England's assistance was superfluous, and that, under the second supposition, it would have proved insufficient. At all events, we know that Spanish gratitude to the English nation was moderate in intensity and short-lived in duration.

CHAPTER XI.

Seventh argument adduced in favour of the old policy.

THAT INTERFERENCE IN EUROPEAN AFFAIRS DOES NOT NECESSARILY EXPOSE US TO THE DANGER OF WAR, BECAUSE WE MAY INTERPOSE OUR MEDIATION WITHOUT BEING COMPELLED TO ENFORCE IT BY PHYSICAL FORCE.

THIS leads us to the analysis of the real meaning of the words "interference," "intervention," "mediation," &c. These terms are unfortunately vague in the extreme, and are constantly used by different people (and sometimes by the same people at different times) in two very opposite senses. They are occasionally intended to signify friendly expostulation, conciliation, suggestions, and counsels tending to heal the breach between the contending parties, and to restore their amicable relations. This course only amounts to pacific mediation, and involves no threat of ulterior consequences should such overtures prove fruitless. But, just as often, the same terms are intended to signify pressing representations and grave remonstrances (as to some line of conduct pursued or likely to be pursued), conveying the alternative of hostile measures in the event of our admonitions being disregarded.

To speak of "intervention" in a general manner without defining (perhaps without considering) the exact signification of the word, and to ignore the wide chasm which separates its two divergent meanings, is a common practice. And as the auditor has perhaps as misty a notion of the term "intervention" as the speaker, the interchange of ideas between them only leads to confusion. Each of the two meanings should have its appropriate expression. The first of them (as above defined) might be enunciated as "pacific mediation," and the second as "armed intervention;" and thus all ambiguity would be avoided.

The advocates for the old policy who use the argument which heads this chapter fall into the error just noticed, and vibrate between the two meanings with convenient elasticity. If they mean "pacific mediation," they give up the point in dispute, as it admits all we contend for. If they mean "armed intervention," it is not true that we do not incur the danger of war : on the contrary, it necessarily implies it as the most probable contingency. But, in fact, they point at something between the two. They are under a vague impression that it is practicable to combine the safety of the former course with the cogency of the latter, by fusing both into the mysterious process of "mediation." They are under a delusion. However enigmatic the language of diplomacy, the statesman with whose policy you interfere will hardly ever fail to discover whether you intend to back your interference by force of arms, or to retire quietly if you meet with a rebuff. If you are understood as coming merely to preach, you will most likely be civilly bowed out. If your mediation bears with it a hostile threat, you will be listened to with far more attention, but the designs which you oppose may be prosecuted in spite of your opposition. In such case, you must be prepared to carry out your threat, and take your place in the battle-field, or resign yourself to the degradation of having held out a menace and shrunk from its execution.

To offer mediation in so ambiguous and evasive a manner as to leave, or rather try to leave, it uncertain whether, in case of its being declined you mean to fight or to retreat, is a shifty expedient which rarely succeeds. It has occasionally happened that the mediating government has not itself quite made up its mind which course it would adopt. This occurred with us under the ministry of the Earl of Aberdeen in 1853, when, after many oscillations, we finally drifted into the war with Russia.

We must, however, estimate the influence of pacific mediation at its true value. It has seldom prevented an impending war when the disputants have been in earnest, but it sometimes hastens the period of reconciliation.

As long as the belligerents are excited by ambition, distrust, or rancour; by hankerings after some supposed advantage, by fears of some apprehended injury, or by indignation at some insult offered ; as long as the hatred and animosities which war fosters as yet transcend all consideration of losses sustained or sacrifices endured, pacific mediation is generally thrust aside with something like contempt. But when the belligerents are sated with carnage, when, through the discomfiture of one or the exhaustion of both, peace becomes almost a necessity ; then, stepping in at the twelfth hour, mediation affords a pretext for negotiation, and may accelerate a pacific issue.

At the same time, nothing can exempt neutrals from the duty of using every effort,— at the slightest opportunity which offers a chance of success,—in spite of every discouragement or rebuff,—however slender the thread of hope,—at whatever sacrifice of apparent dignity (there can

be none of real),—by the proffer again and again
of their good offices,—to put an end to the
miseries and scandal of war. All that is contended for here is that we should form no
exaggerated estimate of the moral influence
through which "pacific mediation" works ; and
above all, that we should clearly comprehend
that, whilst its failure may be probable in the
majority of cases, the apprehension of such
failure by no means justifies any departure from
its recognized limits as a strictly pacific intervention.

There is a mighty influence, increasing still
with the spread of knowledge and freedom,
which works on the decisions of governments
far more powerfully than in former times. We
mean public opinion. It is the audible voice of
the civilized world. It is the exponent of the
average results of all the thoughts of all the
thinkers with regard to the course of public events
and to the acts of public men. It foreshadows
the verdicts of posterity, subject to the correc-
tions derivable from subsequent events and
subsequent acts, and it seldom strays far from
the truth. *Vox populi, vox Dei.* It is rather a
sentiment than a conviction. Its conclusions
are arrived at by intuitive perception rather
than by logical reasoning ; but, like the unerring

E

instincts of the animal creation, it generally points in the right direction. Its vocal organ is the press, through whose myriad channels it conveys its impressions and judgments into the remotest nooks of the civilized world. There is no king or parliament, no statesman or general, but, sooner or later, and more or less must listen to its voice and concede something to its decisions.

When "pacific mediation" has public opinion for an auxiliary, its influence is greatly increased.

Let us illustrate the topic under discussion by a reference to recent events. It has been said that had England "mediated" at the outset of the quarrel between France and Prussia, the late lamentable war might have been avoided.

It cannot be "pacific mediation" that is here meant, for that was freely offered and warmly pressed, but almost scornfully rejected. Fierce rivalry and intense hatred had made both nations eager for the fray, and amidst the din of such tumultuous passions, the whisperings of pacific mediation were scarcely heard and quite unheeded.

It must then be mediation in the sense of "armed intervention" that is meant, and we

ought, under this hypothesis, to have announced
our intention of siding against whichever party
first declared war to the other. Now France
would certainly not have yielded to such a
threat. On the contrary, such an attempt at
dictation on the part of England would have
fanned the flame, and raised the excitement of
the French people to its highest pitch. The
declaration of war against Prussia would have
been hastened, not obviated, and we should thus
have been driven into an alliance with Germany
against France. Need we picture the deplorable
results which would have flowed from such a
position ? Should we not have bitterly repented
the policy of which they would have been the
inevitable consequence ?

CHAPTER XII.

Eighth argument adduced in favour of the old policy.

THAT NON-INTERFERENCE WITH EUROPEAN POLITICS
WOULD NOT PRESERVE US FROM WARS ; AS THEY
WOULD OR MIGHT ORIGINATE IN OTHER SOURCES, SUCH
AS, 1st. GRATUITOUS INSULT OR UNPROVOKED ATTACK
FROM FOREIGN STATES ; 2nd. OUTRAGES ON BRITISH
SUBJECTS FOR WHICH REDRESS WAS REFUSED ; 3rd.
DIFFERENCES BETWEEN OUR OWN VIEWS AND THOSE
OF BELLIGERENTS AS TO OUR DUTIES AS NEUTRALS ;
4th. DISPUTES BETWEEN OUR COLONIES AND FOREIGN
STATES IN WHICH WE MIGHT HAVE TO TAKE A PART.

LET us suppose (for we do not admit) that the
cases stated above come under the category of
inevitable wars, they would at all events, judging
from past history, prove of rare occurrence.
But even if such *casus belli* did occasionally
arise, that could surely be no reason why we
should recklessly engage in a number of wars
which are not inevitable. If there are some
few evils which no foresight or prudence can
avert, that is a poor reason for discarding foresight and prudence, and leaving ourselves exposed to the numerous other evils which they can
avert. Because we may, by the misconduct of
others, be at wide intervals involved in a war

of necessity, such an eventuality cannot relieve us from the duty of bewaring, lest by our own misconduct, we should be plunged into wars which are honourably avoidable.

As to the chances of insult or attack on the part of foreign states, our very abstinence from all wars not justified by self-defence would so tend to husband our national strength, as to render us very formidable foes indeed to those who might venture to assail us. A state that, during a long period of peace and prosperity, (for they are all but inseparable) has laid up a large store of latent power, is far more likely to command respect than to invite attack. It is those states which, avid of military glory, or covetous of increased territory, expend their virile strength till field and city are denuded of their most robust workers, and which distend their pecuniary credit to its utmost verge, by maintaining large standing armies or waging war,—perhaps with apparent success, but certainly with real exhaustion;—it is those states which, at their stage of collapse and reaction, it is safest to insult or attack.

But not only would our avoidance of intermeddling with the affairs of European states make us better able to defend ourselves, but it would render us less liable to offend others.

Whilst it enabled us to accumulate our resources to serve us in time of need, it would keep us aloof from the petty disputes and jealousies which (in the present stage of political knowledge) make Europe a scene of perpetual broils and contentions. Each government is on the watch to overreach and outwit the other. Beneath the conventional courtesies observed in diplomatic intercourse, there frequently lie concealed "hatred, malice, and all uncharitableness."

Treaties generally contain a preamble declaratory of the intentions and motives of the high contracting parties. But their real intentions and motives are quite at variance with the ostensible ones set forth, and the preamble is in most cases a recognized conventional imposture.

Many treaties embrace stipulations to which some one (at least) of the parties is coerced into acceding, either by threats of forcible compulsion, or in consequence of an antecedent exercise of superior physical might. These stipulations, the "high contracting party" in question fully intends to violate at the earliest safe opportunity. When he deems it time to throw off the mask, he announces, in honied words, his profound regret that certain changes in political combinations which have occurred (that do not perhaps in the least modify his treaty obligations), both justify and compel him to, &c. &c.

To steer a straight course amidst the shifting sandbanks, sunken rocks, and devious channels of diplomacy, is utterly impossible, and happy is the nation that shall altogether keep clear of such dangerous navigation.

It is governments, not nations, that have fostered and maintained a normal state of discord and strife throughout Europe. Very few disputes between nation and nation would culminate in war, if, before the governing power had committed itself irretrievably, the suffrage of every adult in the state were taken. It is when a position of defiance has been assumed from which it is impossible to recede without dishonour, and not till then, that the passions of the multitude become inflamed. The producers and distributors of wealth who compose the mass of the community love peace, for their pursuits are peaceful, and their interests suffer from war. But they are not consulted. The rulers decide the question of peace or war, and the people fight and pay. It was ever so, from the oligarchies of Greece and Rome, to the autocracies of modern Europe ; and the words of old Horace might be addressed to the people of the present day. If you, *Achivi*, will submit to be badly governed, then, *quidquid delirant reges*, you must abide by the consequences.

In our country, fortunately, increasing deference is now paid to the popular voice, and in no country in the world, except the United States of America, does public opinion exercise such powerful sway. To this circumstance we owe the growing reluctance of our statesmen to carry out with vigorous consistency the old and still professed policy of interference ; and from it we derive the cheering hope that such policy will, at no distant day, be openly condemned and utterly abandoned. But on the continent of Europe it is otherwise. Government struggles against government, and the people are dragged into the quarrel without being consulted. Of course, the ostensible pretext is the public weal, but the real motive is personal ambition ; for in most European states the aggrandizement and glory of the nation implies the aggrandizement and glory of its governors.

Sometimes mere personal pique is at the bottom of national estrangements. We find in Bulwer's "Life of Lord Palmerston," a curious instance of this in reference to the man who of all others might have been supposed, from his strong sense of duty, to be superior to such a weakness. In 1828, when the Duke of Wellington

was prime minister, he took every opportunity
of thwarting Russia in the settlement of the
question of Greek independence from Turkey.
A similar feeling of personal aversion to Russia
influenced him in all his diplomatic relations
with that power. Bulwer explains this antagonism thus : "The duke is evidently anxious
to break with Russia. He has a strong personal
feeling of dislike to Russia. He has had violent
quarrels with the Lievens, and thought himself
not civilly received at St. Petersburg." So
that we might have been drawn into a war
with Russia to gratify the duke's private resent-
ment.

Sometimes misunderstandings between two
nations have arisen out of a mere breach of
etiquette, or the neglect of some conventional
form between the statesmen who respectively
represented their foreign policy. Bulwer
narrates (vol. ii. p. 222) that at a period when
the French alliance was considered of importance
to us, the Duke of Wellington offended Talleyrand (the French ambassador), by not keeping
appointments, and sometimes making him wait
for one or two hours in the ante-rooms of the
Foreign Office. This led to a coolness between
the two countries, which finally developed itself
in the adoption of a divergent policy. On such

miserable trifles has depended the question of friendship or hostility between millions of human beings.

Lord Palmerston was one of the most zealous, active, and successful votaries of the system of interference, and has left us a fatal legacy of certain strife and probable wars by his multifarious and complicated treaties, conventions, alliances, co-guarantees, &c., in every part of Europe. His intervention extended over Portugal, Spain, Belgium, Rome, Greece, Turkey, Egypt, and Circassia. He entangled us into a partnership with a number of weak and petty states, and inflicted on us the burthen of maintaining their tottering existence, just as banks are sometimes induced (generally to their ruin) to bolster up insolvent commercial firms. He was always at work, encouraging one party, threatening the other, conciliating the strong, influencing the weak ; and these manœuvres, when they did not plunge us into actual war, kept us continually on the brink of one, and compelled England to expend enormous sums in warlike preparations and demonstrations.

Not only, by a policy of isolation, would the possible grounds for war become very few instead of being very many, but those few would be easily susceptible of friendly settlement. If our future relations with foreign states should be exempt from the old teeming sources of irritation and jealousies, there would be little difficulty in an amicable adjustment of the minor incidents which have been alluded to as possible grounds of collision under the system of non-intervention.

The United States of America have uniformly acted on the policy here advocated, and have never received from other states any slight or molestation whatever. Nor are they likely to have any differences which friendly discussion, or at most, arbitration, may not bring to a peaceable issue. There is no reason why the adoption by England of a similar policy should not lead to the same results.

It may be said that the great distance of New York from Europe makes all the difference. Measured by miles, the difference is great, but it is not so in respect to political combinations or hostile operations. The introduction of steam has brought the shores of America practically nearer to Europe than those of England were to Brest or Antwerp formerly, when the uncertain winds were the only locomotive power for ships of war. The United States are as accessible now to hostile fleets as we were then ; and if exposure to attack is a good plea for meddling with the affairs of other states, that plea is as valid to-day for our transatlantic brethren as it was for us fifty years ago. If their policy is a wise one, ours must have been a mistake.

The narrow sea which separates us from the Continent isolates us as practically as though it were decupled in width. If distance be assumed as the element that is to decide the nature of our political relations with Europe, then let us suppose these islands shifted two hundred miles to the west; would this change of geographical position be sufficient to subvert those relations? Would it be contended that a foreign policy similar to that of the United States would be beneficial for us then whilst inexpedient now? And if two hundred miles would make all the difference, would a hundred? would fifty? Where is the line to be drawn?

If under the *régime* of non-intervention, a dispute with some power were, against all probability, to arise in which we were, or thought we were, in the right, and which our efforts at amicable arrangement or our offers of adjustment by arbitration failed to bring to a peaceful issue, then such a case would clearly come under the category of a just and necessary war. To the conduct of such a war we should bring our undivided energies, and our accumulated and unwasted strength. We should, in addition, be sustained not only by the public conscience of England, but by the public opinion of the civilized world. With such odds in our favour, over and above our intrinsic strength, discomfiture would be very unlikely.

———•———

CHAPTER XIII.

Ninth argument adduced in favour of the old policy.

THAT WITHOUT OCCASIONAL WARS THE NATION MIGHT LOSE ITS MARTIAL PROWESS, AND SINK INTO EFFEMINACY; THAT WE SHOULD FORFEIT OUR MARITIME SUPREMACY; THAT OUR NAVAL AND MILITARY ESTABLISHMENTS WOULD BE SO REDUCED, AS TO COURT ATTACKS WHICH WE SHOULD BE POWERLESS TO REPEL.

THIS objection starts *in limine* with a contradiction in terms. It supposes, at the same time, that wars will *not* occur, whence it argues our military decadency; and that wars *will* occur, to which our military decadency arising from the absence of war will render us unequal.

It however suggests several topics which may deserve some notice.

Whether the infrequency of war impairs the martial prowess of a nation, is a question for the solution of which we unfortunately possess few data. For there are few regions in Europe in which there has not been a nearly constant succession of wars, especially since the spread of civilization. Perhaps the countries which have been engaged in the fewest military contests are Sweden and Denmark, for want of opportunities ; Switzerland (whose inhabitants have made up for it by enlisting as mercenaries)—and Russia, probably because she emerged from barbarism at a later period, and did not belong to the "great European family" till the reign of Peter. These instances, however, seem to tell the other way, as no one can impute effeminacy to the Swedes, Danes, Swiss, and Russians.

The United States have engaged in very few wars, with the exception of petty conflicts with Mexicans and aboriginal Indians ; yet when a serious struggle survened between the northern and southern states, the courage, resources, and military skill exhibited on both sides were never surpassed.

The proposition, therefore, as to peaceable nations losing their " martial prowess," is, to say the least, totally devoid of proof.

Moreover, war is becoming every year less a matter of personal valour than a matter of organization, science, and money. Hand to hand fights are now rare, except in slight skirmishes, which decide nothing. Final victory is the

reward of that belligerent which by means of the
most systematic application of the most scientific
improvements, and of a well organized and
abundant commissariat, moves large masses on a
given point with the greatest celerity and precision, and supports them with the most powerful
artillery, constructed and mounted on the most
effective principles. Battles are won by machines
—machines in the shape of "arms of precision,"
which are loaded, pointed, and fired by machines
in the shape of men. Mere pluck and muscle,
which formerly carried all before them, are now
of little value beyond endowing soldiers with
powers of endurance, passive indifference to
danger, and physical capacity for long marches.
In the Franco-Prussian war not a fortress was
stormed. All the strong places were reduced
either by the play of artillery, or by stress of
famine. Bayonets were seldom crossed, and not
a single important battle was decided by individual prowess.

To embark into war in order to foster the
martial spirit of a nation, ever was, and is now,
more than ever, a costly and immoral means to
an useless end.

As to our "maritime supremacy," it seems
to be regarded by many in the light of a position
meekly acquiesced in by other nations, entitling

us to some peculiar undisputed privileges, which we should forfeit by adopting a peaceful policy. But our "maritime supremacy" has never meant more than the appreciation by foreign states of our naval strength, and of the skill and courage of our sailors. There is no reason why we should, by a change of policy, lose one jot of that appreciation. The strength of our navy need not suffer diminution, and as to the gallantry of our sailors, why should that be impaired? With a peaceful policy which secures the undisturbed development and extension of our trade, our commercial navy would receive constant accession. Now, though a nation spend countless treasure in building any number of war-ships, these, when put to the test, will prove mere toys, if not manned by hardy, well-trained, and experienced crews. Such crews are utterly unobtainable in adequate numbers, unless recruited from a large commercial navy. That copious nursery for competent mariners we shall always possess as long as our increasing commerce gives employment to increasing fleets of merchant vessels. This circumstance of itself would suffice to preserve to us that pre-eminent position as a naval power which is all that can be meant by that vague locution, "maritime supremacy."

In the minds of some men there lurks the notion that our "maritime supremacy" can only be maintained by allowing no other navy to grow into formidable dimensions. To this end, we are to seize any pretext for going to war with a rising maritime power, whilst we are yet the stronger, and crush our prospective rival by destroying his fleets before he becomes dangerous. The process if carried out would doubtless be a short cut to the end aimed at ; but it is so flagrantly immoral, so uncertain of accomplishment, so likely to be retorted on us should we fail of success, so redolent of the old barbarous policy of regarding it as the height of prosperity to mar the prosperity of others—it so utterly recognizes the sovereignty of brute force, and so cynically ignores all question of right and wrong, —that no words need be wasted in a formal refutation of so preposterous a scheme.

It by no means follows that, our chances of permanent peace being immeasurably increased by our abstinence from participation in the petty feuds of European states, therefore our military and naval establishments should be immediately reduced. It is true that we might probably conclude, after sufficient experience of the new policy, that we could leave in the pockets of our people a portion of what we now

F

spend in warlike preparations, but, at first, the
community might deem it prudent to be fully
prepared for all contingencies. At all events,
every additional year of peace would supply us
with additional resources to meet war, should it
come. As a nation becomes wealthier, not only
can it afford to expend more on armies, navies,
artillery, fortifications, &c., but it is able to bear
the strain for a longer period. Unless we go
back to the times of the Huns and Vandals, and
conduct war with the same primitive weapons, a
poor nation has no chance against a rich one. In
modern warfare, wealth is power, and the financial
question underlies every military operation.

Unfortunately for the interests of peace,
modern nations spend in war, not only the
utmost they can afford out of their present
capital, but they mortgage their future earnings
and those of their posterity, in order to indulge
in that cruel luxury. Like desperate gamblers,
besides losing their ready money, they contract
ruinous obligations, which cripple them and their
heirs for ever after.

Our own ancestors were the first to discover,
with fatal ingenuity, that by incurring a national
debt, armaments could be increased, wars pro-
longed, and the burthen shifted on to succeeding
generations. The lesson was not lost on other

states, and although we have retained the foremost rank in the scale of indebtedness, there is
scarcely a civilised nation whose people have
not to give up a portion of their hard earnings
to pay interest on borrowed money, most of
which was spent before they were born, in unjust
and unnecessary wars.*

As, however, every abuse when it reaches its
maximum creates reaction, so it may be hoped
that the borrowing power of nations will before
long reach its final limit. As a state goes on
accumulating loan upon loan, the time will
come when the interest annually payable will
cause so intolerable a strain on the industrial
resources of the country, that it will either
cease to be paid, or it will be reduced in
amount by some compromise with the national
creditors. When that day arrives, lenders will
no longer be so easily found, and loans will
either be totally unobtainable, or if obtained,
it will only be on usurious terms and for
limited amounts. The financial collapse of a
state must necessarily cripple its military power;
and just as a spendthrift reforms perforce

---

* One glorious exception is the loan of £20,000,000 contracted by England in 1833, to redeem the slaves held by her
West India colonists, but this is a mere fractional part of the
£800,000,000 we then owed. A very small quantity of " bread "
to an intolerable deal of " sack !"

when his money and credit are both exhausted, so nations may be compelled to remain at peace through sheer inability to wage war. Whether that state of things be distant or not, we are nearing it, and those countries which are the most warlike, and in that sense the most powerful, are travelling towards it with the greatest rapidity.

It is therefore incontestable that our ability to carry on hostile operations with vigour, whenever war should be forced upon us, will be great in proportion to our persistent abstinence from unnecessary wars ; and that as to those states which are ambitious of military glory, the more frequent their very triumphs, the more thickly will the seeds of future decay be sown, and the more rapidly will they germinate.

That a neutral and peaceful attitude on our part might induce continental powers to combine for the purpose of attacking us, is a notion totally opposed to experience and common sense. Our retirement from the intrigues and complications of European policy would allay those feelings of jealousy, mistrust, and ill-will, which have always been, and must always be, engendered by the system of intervention on which we have hitherto acted. How can the removal of almost every possible cause of dispute

tend to court hostility ?   Not only would pretexts
be more and more difficult to invent, but all
inducement would be wanting—nay, there would
be strong inducements the other way.   For what
could continental nations gain by wantonly and
gratuitously attacking us ?   Our still increasing
wealth and prosperity might excite their envy,
but wealth and prosperity are not possessions to
be transferred by force of arms from one country
to another.   Absurd as are the occasional freaks
of military powers, a totally objectless war can
hardly be deemed within the bounds of probability.   On the other hand, there would exist many
inducements to leave us undisturbed in our isolation. Continental Europe would remain what it has
always been, an arena for political gladiatorship.
Each leading state would continue to display
avidity for its own aggrandizement, and jealousy
of the aggrandizement of others. Alliances would,
no doubt, still be contracted which a sudden
turn in affairs would convert into enmities ; the
horrors of war would still periodically transform
provinces into deserts, and leave, under the veil
of an illusory peace, deadly animosities to develop
themselves into future wars ; large standing
armies would still take the workers away from
the plough and the loom, and turn them into
unproductive consumers ; in fine, Europe would

continue to be a scene of discord and strife, of hollow alliances and fragile treaties. It is not out of these elements of confusion and wrangling that a combination against a powerful country is likely to arise without a plausible pretext, and without a definite object.

European states do not combine against the United States of America; and yet, supposing us released from continental entanglements, the circumstances would become exactly parallel. If, in their case, all fear of unprovoked attacks is an idle dream, so it would be in ours. The mighty republic of the new world is not considered a third-rate power, or taxed with want of influence or *prestige* because it does not interfere with the petty quarrels of the old, effete, and stagnant nations of Europe; and if we had the moral courage to proclaim the same policy, we should occupy the same position.

Probably, when it shall become patent that we had withdrawn our stakes from the losing game of European politics, we may be twitted by excited pamphleteers with having lost all our continental influence, and dropped into the rank of a third-rate power. We could, however, well afford to smile at those stingless taunts of which the authors themselves would know the absurdity. As to losing our "continental influence," it will be a good riddance, as it has only served to involve us in expensive wars for the sake of other states ; and our rank in the scale of nations depends, not on loose epithets unjustified by facts, but on our substantial power, which would be greater than ever.

Whatever might be said or written, we should be credited with having adopted the best course, and we should enjoy the real benefits of increased material power and increased moral influence.

The necessity of occasional wars, to prevent Englishmen from sinking into effeminacy has, in some quarters, been feebly alleged, but a moment's consideration suffices for its disproof. Forty years of peace had not impaired the courage and endurance of the men of Inkermann, and the heroic deeds performed by our countrymen during the Indian mutiny certainly evinced no degeneracy in our lineage.

Englishmen have always (whether in time of peace or in time of war) been passionately fond of, and addicted to, country sports (hunting, shooting, cricket, &c.), athletic exercises, open-air games, mountain climbing, yachting, adventurous explorations, &c. A people in whom such habits have taken deep root do not fall into effeminacy. The sailors who fought in Syria, under Napier, or who explored the Arctic Seas under Ross and McClintock, were worthy scions of the men through whose gallantry Rodney and Nelson won their laurels. A long period of peace has never yet quenched the spirit of Englishmen, and we believe it never would.

In fact, the tendencies run precisely in a contrary direction. It is warlike nations that suffer from degeneracy. War, and preparations for war, in the shape of large standing armies, displace the flower of the people, the strongest, healthiest, best formed men in their prime, from their legitimate position as fathers of families, and impair their health and vigour by bodily injuries or mutilation, by exhaustion from over-exertion, by exposure to inclement weather, or by licentious habits contracted in the camp. The consequence is a gradual deterioration in the race, and where the cause operates on a large scale, and for generation after generation, the result is a people of stunted growth and enfeebled constitution :—

> " Ætas parentum, pejor avis, tulit
> Nos nequiores, mox daturos
> Progeniem vitiosiorem."

This is a subject to which we can do no more than allude here, but which is well worthy of careful investigation on the part of physiological and statistical inquirers.

CHAPTER XIV.

Tenth argument adduced in favour of the old policy.

THAT OLD ALLIANCES AND EXISTING TREATIES TO WHICH WE ARE STILL BOUND PREVENT THE ADOPTION OF THE POLICY OF ISOLATION ADVOCATED IN THIS ESSAY.

IN urging a policy of self-dependence and isolation, it is by no means intended to suggest that we should withdraw from a single obligation to which we are bound, or shrink from any responsibility which our predecessors have incurred. The course recommended is simply to let those liabilities live out their natural term, and neither to renew them nor replace them by others. From the following considerations it will appear highly probable that we should not have to wait very long before we were totally extricated from our existing entanglements, either by efflux of time or by the natural course of events.

In the case of commercial treaties, postal conventions, &c., they are almost always concluded for a term of years, on the expiry of which it is optional with the contracting parties to renew them or not. National compacts of this class present, therefore, no difficulties.

Alliances and coalitions between two or more states are frequently entered into for the accomplishment of some special object, which, when attained, or when recognized as unattainable, the alliance dies a natural death. Alliances which do not come under the above category are mostly merged into treaties which enumerate the respective obligations of each party towards the remainder.

Treaties may be divided into two principal classes :—1st. Those into which all the contracting parties enter voluntarily and without extrinsic pressure. 2nd. Those into which one at least of the co-signitaries is coerced, either by the result of an unsuccessful war, or by the dread of provoking an unequal contest.

Treaties which come under either class, but especially those which come under the second, though professedly ranging over an indefinite future, fall sooner or later into desuetude, and silently fade into nullity by repeated and unresisted infractions. Like the three truces of fifty years each that made an old man of Wamba, the son of Witless, these perennial treaties become, after a time, mere waste paper. New political combinations, changes in the internal constitution of some of the parties, a collapse in the power of one state, the expansion of the power of another, and a variety of circumstances tending to alter the relative position of one or more of the contracting parties to the rest, gradually loosen and finally disrupt the ties which bind them together. The compact becomes null and void, and with it, the obligations which it comprised. When a treaty has become obsolete, or when all the parties to it concur of their own free will (however divergent their several motives) in abrogating it, each is at liberty to adopt or to reject any proposition that may be made for its renewal or replacement. It is through the operation of this law of change that England may, honourably and justly, disengage herself gradually from the meshes in which the old meddling diplomacy has entangled her.

It must be borne in mind that England entered into no alliances, treaties, or coalitions, unless from motives founded, ostensibly at least, on considerations of national expediency. We never went to war "for an idea." Nor can any blame be cast on our past rulers for having discarded all professions of abstract philanthropy, and only consulted what they deemed to be the interests of their country. But we consider .their views as to the true interests of the country to have been erroneous. We quite agree that the honour and welfare of the com-

munity constitute the sole objects of a statesman's solicitude, but we contend that the old
policy leads us away from, instead of leading us
towards those objects. The principle which
prompted former governments to take an active
part in European intrigues, is the same which,
after long and bitter experience, should induce us
to refrain. Our predecessors joined other states
in expensive and dangerous undertakings, for
objects which we consider to have been mostly
illusory or unattainable, and all but worthless
even if attained. From so losing a venture we
desire to withdraw our stake, if we can do so
honourably ; but certainly when the game is
fairly over we may decline playing any more.

It is true that our outstanding engagements
may, before they cease and determine, place us
in such a position as to make war unavoidable.
Such a calamity is quite possible, and from
the responsibility we must not shrink. It would
no doubt prove a grievous misfortune, and all
the more grievous that we disapproved of the
policy that drove us into it. But nations do not
die like individuals. They have a continuous
existence, and we are bound by the acts of our
pre-existing governments. As we inherit the
status of our forefathers, so we inherit their
obligations ; for if it were once admitted as a

principle that a government might repudiate the compacts entered into by preceding governments, there would be an end to all international arrangements. Melancholy as the alternative might be, we should be compelled (if needful) to shed our blood, waste our treasures, and expend our energies in discharge of the bond to which we were vicarious parties. Some good, however, might arise out of the evil. We might derive from it a keener apprehension of the errors of a policy that had conduced to so sinister a result, and a firmer determination to avoid them.

But whilst recognizing the responsibilities entailed on us by past treaties, so long as these endure in their integrity, it is essential that, in all negociations connected with them, we should bear in mind our determination (should we so determine) neither to renew nor replace them. There should be no trimming between the two courses. If our future foreign policy is to be based on a system of isolation, our diplomacy must shape its path directly and unswervingly towards that end.

A shifty and wavering policy never commanded respect. If we are to be the policemen of Europe, let us act the part with vigour. Or, if we find the work to be unpleasant and decidedly underpaid, let us quit the *corps*. But

to assume the office and evade its duties is, to
say the least of it, undignified. It subjects us
to the imputation of letting "I dare not wait
upon I would," and nothing is more con-
temptible than half-threats backed by half-
measures, dwindling into torpid quiescence.

Moreover, a vacillating policy is unjust towards
those minor states of Europe which have been
accustomed to look for our interference on their
behalf in cases of emergency, not from any
express treaty-stipulations, but from the habitual
drift of our old traditional policy, which rendered
such interference probable. Relying in a measure
on the chance of our support (a support which
we sometimes afforded and sometimes denied),
these states are tempted into taking up positions
which, alone and unaided, they are unable to
maintain, and led into dangers for which they
therefore hold us morally responsible.

CHAPTER XV.

*Search after more arguments adducible in favour
of the old policy.*

EVERY effort has been made to muster in the
preceding chapters all the arguments that are,
or could be, adduced in favour of the old policy.

On ransacking the works and marshalling the allegations of the best writers and speakers on the subject, no additional topics have been elicited beyond those already discussed. It may be well, however, to advert to the principles propounded within a recent period, by two very able men, in reference to this question.

Lord Palmerston declared the three fundamental points of his foreign policy to be :—1st, the interests of England ; 2nd, the balance of power; and 3rd, the maintenance of peace in Europe. These propositions we have already fully discussed, but to save reference to previous pages, our conclusions with regard to each may be concisely repeated. 1st. The interests of England require peace, and are injured by war or the apprehension of war. 2nd. The balance of power has proved an "*ignis fatuus*," that has enticed our statesmen into bogs and quagmires, and the pursuit of it has cost millions of lives and hundreds of millions of money, whilst it has still remained unclutched and intangible. 3rd. Peace is jeopardized, not promoted, by threatening with forcible intervention those states which refuse to coincide with our views, and to accede to our conditions.

Palmerston's warm admirer, Sir H. Bulwer (now Lord Dalling), advocates the policy of in-

t erference ("Life of Lord Palmerston," Vol. II.
pp. 218-9) on the following grounds, to which
we shall take the liberty of intercalating a
running commentary.   1st. Because it is required
by our vast commercial relations. (They only
require to be "let alone," and dissensions with
foreign nations are in the highest degree pre-
judicial to them.)   2nd. Because we are one of a
community of nations, and ought therefore to act
as an individual forming a community of individuals. (Individuals do form an organized community, and are bound to obey its laws ; but
nations do not form a community, and are amen-
able to no extrinsic earthly tribunal.) 3rd. Because
we ought not to be inert when other states pursue
a system hostile to our ideas and institutions. (A
good reason for every nation making war on every
other nation ; for each state pursues its own
system, which is mostly "hostile to the ideas
and institutions" of the rest ; but a general war
would be an undeniable evil.) 4th. Because we
ought to act on principles as principles, and not
simply in respect to their application to our own
property and safety. (This is the argument used
by religious persecutors on the one hand, and by
the red republicans on the other.   Are we so
infallible that our principles must necessarily be
the only right principles ?   And are we justified

in cramming them down the throats of others at
the point of the bayonet?) 5th. Because we ought
to imitate society, which combines against murder
and theft. (War is frequently theft and always
murder, but nations do not combine against either
as society does against both. Society is knit together by common interests, whilst nations are dis-
severed by antagonistic purposes, and the cases
are not at all parallel. For instance, if Spain were
to try to wrest Gibraltar from us, would the "great
European family" combine with us to resist
so nefarious an attempt? Most probably not.)
6th. As a man is amongst men, so is a state
amongst states. (This is merely a repetition of
allegation 2.)

It is but right to add, that whilst controverting
the political views of the two statesmen referred
to, we cast no doubt on the sincerity of their con-
victions, nor entertain any but the highest opinion
of their ability and honesty.

———◆———

CHAPTER XVI.

The general advantages of a policy of isolation.

THE chief benefits of a policy of isolation
consist in immunity from the manifold evils
which have resulted from the contrary system

G

during its long prevalence. In our strictures
upon the alleged advantages of the policy of
interference, the two systems have been so fully
contrasted, that the beneficial consequences
which are expected to flow from the change
advocated, have been distinctly brought to
view. To escape from evil is in itself a
boon. Just as trade flourishes best when not
nursed or protected (as it is called) by legis-
lative enactments, so will our foreign relations
be in their happiest position when freed from the
burdensome assistance of treaties and alliances.
We may be friends with our neighbours, and yet
abjure all partnership with them. Surely we
have grave social problems enough to solve
at home, to occupy the utmost stretch of our
intellects, without going abroad to settle the
affairs of other nations.

Even if it could be shown that, at some
antecedent period, it was useful or expedient to
adopt a policy of interference (a very questionable proposition), it does not follow that the
same system is applicable to existing circumstances. Within the last century radical changes
have taken place in matters deeply affecting the
future destinies of the human race. Passing by
such comparative trifles as the fall of dynasties,
and alterations of a few hundred square miles in

the respective boundaries of European states, let us consider the far more momentous and lasting changes introduced, and still being introduced, by the following agencies :—

1st. The rapid increase in the population, wealth, and power of the American, Australian, and other nationalities originally founded by us, and still composed of the Anglo-Saxon race; the steady, though far less luxuriant growth of the Brazilian empire and the South American republics; and the newly-opened communication with three hundred or four hundred millions of human beings in China and Japan. These are circumstances which must naturally tend to divert our attention from Europe. Our daily extending intercourse with those great countries, some of which already comprise one-third of the entire population of the globe, whilst others possess almost limitless scope for development, must more and more loosen our ties with European states, which, cooped up in their small confines, have almost reached their utmost limit of growth.

2nd. The increased facilities for locomotion by means of steam, and for intercommunication by means of the electric telegraph. These have so shortened distances, as practically to contract the surface of the habitable globe within comparatively small dimensions. All arguments, founded

on mere proximity, for adopting one line of
policy with European powers, and another with
American and Asiatic states, are thereby an-
nulled.

3rd. The increased power, by means of scientific appliances, of producing and distributing
commodities serviceable to man. This beneficent power, whilst it showers down blessings on
the world at large, and brings all the nations of
the world into closer contact, tends to isolate
Europe, which, ignoring free trade, persists in
moving in a little orbit of its own.

4th. The increased freedom of inquiry amongst
all classes and on all subjects. It shrinks from
no topic, however delicate, and raises questions
affecting the very foundations of the present
fabric of society ; such as the claims of the
wage-receivers to a larger share than they now
obtain of the wealth which they help to create
—the tenure of land—the supposed antagonism
between capital and labour —and all the other
socialistic theories down to communism, which
seeks to abolish altogether the right of individuals to hold property. These speculations,
which full and free discussion will eventually
reduce to their true value, meanwhile so un-
settle the opinions, and so influence the pro-
ceedings, of large masses of men throughout

Europe, that they greatly complicate our international relations with their respective governments.

To apply to these altered circumstances an unaltered rule of action, is to ignore passing events, and to resort to easy routine as a substitute for hard logic.

The utmost efforts of our highest intellects are now directed to the removal from amongst us of pauperism, disease, and discontent, as far as human efforts may avail. But their task is a laborious one. Just as increased knowledge shows us how little we know, and how much remains to be known, so, whatever social improvements we have made serve to show us how little we have improved, and how vast a scope there still exists for further advance.

At all events it must be admitted that the suspension of social progress is a very serious addition to the many other enormous calamities of war.

The national benefits that would accrue from a policy of isolation have been amply elicited in the course of our previous criticisms on the opposite policy. It may, however, be well to allude succinctly to a few of the more salient advantages which it promises.

CHAPTER XVII.

First argument in favour of the policy of isolation.

AVOIDANCE OF UNNECESSARY WARS.

IF this were the sole argument producible in favour of the new policy, it would be quite sufficient to insure its acceptance. There is something so barbarous, and hence unreasonable, and something so unreasonable, and therefore barbarous, in the idea of brute force settling questions of right or wrong, that common sense revolts against it. But man is a compound being. Whilst the spiritual element keeps the mastery, the slaying of a fellow creature is considered as a crime of the deepest dye, and intolerable remorse pursues the murderer to his grave. On the other hand, when the animal element gains the ascendancy, no wolf is so ravenous for slaughter. The shedding of blood maddens the blood-shedder, and creates a morbid thirst for more. The very intellect of man, which constitutes him an improvable and responsible being, is made to minister to his evil passions. Science, with cruel impartiality, develops man's power over the elements for evil as well as for good purposes. With equal readi-

ness it ministers to our comforts, and extends
our knowledge of Nature's laws, or invents instruments that shall scatter death more pro-
fusely in one day than the blackest plague has
ever done in a year. It helps to manufacture
cheap calico, and constructs *mitrailleuses.* It is
not that science is to blame. Its mission is
simply to investigate the laws of Nature, and
point out in what manner they may subserve
man's purposes, good or bad. For the vicious
use of the knowledge so acquired and imparted
science is not responsible.

In modern wars there are not the same opportunities as formerly for the pacific intervention
of neutrals. Previous to the innovations in the
art of war introduced by the first Napoleon,
armies were much smaller, and the instruments
of destruction less efficient than they are now.
The battles were indecisive, and the operations
consisted mainly of marches, countermarches,
and tactical manœuvres. Winter separated the
combatants, and from November to March the
troops were comfortably ensconced in their
respective winter quarters. Meanwhile, negotia-
tions phlegmatically proceeded ; national antipathies did not kindle into burning hatred ;
neutrals coolly looked on, or interfered either in
a mild or in a moderately forcible way ; and

the wars were more protracted, but far less
sanguinary. But now, *nous avons changé tout
cela.* Enormous masses of armed men, to
which the armies of Turenne, or even of Wellington, would have been reckoned as small
detachments, meet in deadly conflict, and in
a few hours acres of ground are strewed with
thousands of dead bodies, probably equalling in
number the male adult population of a moderate-
sized city—let us say York. Thus wars have
become short but very sharp. The work of
carnage goes on winter as well as summer,
and "panting" diplomacy "toils after it in
vain."

Everybody admits—indeed loudly declares—
that war is a "blunder as well as a crime;" but,
whilst everybody preaches, no practical step is
taken. There prevails a vague, dreamy impression, that war is a "necessary evil." That
it is an evil, yes, decidedly; but that it is
necessary, we deny. The policy broached in
these pages affords us an opportunity of acting up
to our professions as to the wickedness of war.
Let us cut adrift from Europe, and devote ourselves to the welfare of the members of our own
community. If all nations did the same, the
greatest obstacle to the real progress of mankind would be removed. Let us at least set the

example. To say, "war is a disgrace to humanity and civilization," and in the same breath to say, " Let us wage war with Russia, to prevent her from incorporating Wallachia," is a gross inconsistency, and can only imply that our professed detestation of war is unreal, and our sententious condemnation of it hypocrisy.

———•———

CHAPTER XVIII.

Second argument in favour of the policy of isolation.

REMOVAL OF THE INCONVENIENCES ATTENDING— 1st. A LARGE STANDING ARMY. 2nd. COSTLY WARLIKE PREPARATIONS. 3rd. THE SUSPENSION OF INTERNAL IMPROVEMENTS ON ACCOUNT OF EXTERNAL POLITICAL COMPLICATIONS.

IT is by no means contended that a standing army and fair stores of warlike appliances would not be required if we abstained from admixture with continental politics. Even when we have nothing to apprehend from open assailants, it is proper to guard ourselves from the possible attacks of unprovoked marauders. However mighty our latent strength, some portion of our force must be in immediate readi-

ness, if only as a nucleus for further enlargement
in case of necessity.

But the scale of expenditure requisite for a
defensive war is a mere trifle compared with
that indispensable in the event of a war that
has to be waged in distant lands, such as Spain,
Italy, or Turkey.

Moreover, the chance of our being attacked,
when our policy offers no .pretext for it, is infinitesimal as compared with the probabilities of
a war as long as we continue mixed up with a
complex system, which is yearly undergoing
changes and modifications involving either our
tacit acquiescence or our active opposition.

A nation as wealthy as ours could without
the slightest strain bear the moderate burden
requisite to make ourselves respected, as long as
we abstained from the absurd pretension to
compel other nations to conform to our notions
of what they ought or ought not to do.

The mission of governments is to provide the
means of affording security to the lives and
property of the people governed. When that
object can only be obtained by an appeal to
arms, then, and then alone, war is just and
necessary. But a list of the wars waged by
England for the last two centuries would show
that scarcely any of them answered that de-

scription. Almost all have originated in improper interference with the affairs of other people. History, by proving the infrequency of just and necessary wars, makes it clear that if those should be the only wars we were to engage in, the present scale of our armaments might, with perfect safety, be notably reduced.

One of the greatest benefits that would accrue from the infrequency of war is the opportunity which it would give us of proceeding, without interruption, with internal reforms. From these our attention is now distracted by every rumour of war between other states, and by the possibility of our being entangled in it by old treaty-liabilities. Inchoate measures of improvement are abandoned. If an independent member of parliament should offer some useful suggestion, he is met by the stereotyped reply, "The proposition may be good in itself, but the moment is inopportune." We stop improving and begin spending. The storm may blow over, but the expense has to be met, and the task of improvement to be recommenced. The removal of this grave inconvenience would be hailed with gratification by every well-wisher to his country.

CHAPTER XIX.

Third argument in favour of a policy of isolation.

THE CESSATION OF JEALOUSY AND DISTRUST ON THE
PART OF FOREIGN STATES.

As long as we profess adherence to the old
traditional policy, our relations with other states
are in a constant state of ferment. In every
fresh combination which time infallibly brings
about, we are found to be the great obstacles to
change. We are parties to some old treaty that
upholds an antiquated state of things, and we
stand in the way. One of the contending powers
hopes, and the other fears, that we may prove
obstinate. Sometimes we give way, and then
the hopes, being disappointed, change into
rancour ; and the fears, being unrealised, subside
into something like contempt. But sometimes
we resist, and then we have to stand the brunt
of war, with all its deplorable consequences.

Indeed, with our present complex treaty-
system, it is no exaggeration to say that we are
never in a thorough state of peace. In virtue of
our obligations under guarantee treaties, we are
practically at war with the states against whose
possible encroachments those treaties are di-

rected. If not engaged in actual hostilities
against them, we are respectively in a state of
chronic antagonism. By holding them to a
certain line of conduct by the threat of armed
interference, we leave it in their power at any
moment to plunge us into war by adopting the
course which we have prohibited. Can this be
called a state of peace ?

Several causes for the jealousy of foreign states
will continue to exist so long as we continue to
intermeddle with European politics, besides the
mere fact of our interfering with their international arrangements. We do not get credit
for the disinterestedness which we profess.
That our intervention proceeds from no other
motives than a wish to maintain the " balance of
power," and that it is out of sheer philanthropy
that we resort to threats and even to main force
to compel one state to keep the peace towards
another, or to rescue the vanquished from the
consequences of defeat, are pleas which men
listen to with utter incredulity. The world
considers them to be mere pretexts, and ascribes
our movements to selfish schemes of aggrandizement. Indeed, our conduct has generally tended
to justify such scepticism on the part of the
world. We have from time to time used our
maritime preponderance to increase our pos-

sessions in every quarter of the globe. Besides the legitimate expansion of our empire by colonization, we have taken and retained possession of snug islands and important strongholds. Amongst the latter we may instance Gibraltar and Malta, the acquisition of which, and the strong grasp we still maintain on them, seem rather inconsistent with professions of self-denial.

But whenever we thoroughly retire from the European arena of strife and contention, and make it patent to other states that we neither seek to interfere with them nor to secure territorial gains for ourselves, we shall at once put an end to every cause for jealousy and mistrust on their part, and permanent peace may at last become a reality.

CHAPTER XX.

Fourth argument in favour of a policy of isolation.

IT WOULD CONDUCE TO, AND FACILITATE, THE SETTLEMENT OF INTERNATIONAL DISPUTES BY ARBITRATION.

ONE of the main obstacles to the adoption of arbitration as a mode of settling disputes between two nations, is the difficulty of finding an intermediate government which, whilst it occupies a rank suitable to so important a function, has no interests, direct or indirect, in the question at issue, and is therefore free from all bias, or suspicion of bias. The tangled ramifications of diplomacy have so interlaced each European power with the rest, that no single one is quite exempt from the presumption of nurturing, from egotistical motives, an undue preference towards one or the other of the parties in dispute. A strong state is mistrusted as entertaining designs; a weak state as influenced by fears. But England, aloof from all European concerns, known, therefore, to entertain no selfish designs, and unimpressible by fears, would readily be accepted as referee between contending governments, and her awards would be received with deference and respect.

All other states adopting the same policy would be eligible to the same honourable functions, till at last there would remain no defensible pretext for refusing to refer national disputes to the arbitrament of independent and disinterested neutrals.

Several other incidental benefits would accrue from our isolation, and consequent impartiality. Amongst other important questions which would be affected by these beneficial influences, we may refer to :—

1st. Free trade—which is to commerce what mountain air is to human beings, as compared with the vitiated atmosphere of dungeons or theatres—might then be canvassed on its own merits or demerits, and dissociated from political considerations with which, intrinsically, it has nothing whatever to do. Napoleon's Berlin decrees inflicted great losses on millions of his friends on the continent, with a view to inflict injury on England. But this embargo on the natural liberty of barter between man and man caused infinite distress without accomplishing the political objects it was intended to achieve. Napoleon's device has, however, not been without its imitators. The prohibitory system is only a politer form of the Berlin decrees, and its *raison d'etre* is, in many cases, less commercial than political. The class interests which pro-tection fosters at the expense of the community at large, and which, like theatres in France, are subsidized by the nation, would have much less weight were it not for their convenient subser-vience to the political fears or antipathies of the governing power. To remove those fears and antipathies is one of the main objects of the policy here advocated.

2nd. The importance of clearly defining, once for all, the duties and rights of neutrals, and fixing on a precise code of international law, is admitted on all hands ; and yet our parliamentary discussions on those subjects chiefly hinge on the somewhat vague and contradictory doctrines laid down, nearly two centuries ago, in the antiquated works of Vattel, Grotius, Puffendorf, and Cornelius van Bynkershoeck,* a quotation from whose pages is gravely expected to have nearly the force of law.

A congress, to which each civilised state appointed a representative, might settle all such questions for ever, in the course of a few weeks. But while common sense suggests so easy a solution of so great a difficulty, national rivalries interpose an insuperable bar. If, however, England once stood above all suspicion of harbouring sinister designs against other states, her initiation of such a congress during an

* Cornelius Van Bynkershoeck being once quoted in parliament by George Canning, the oddity of the name induced the members to fancy that it was a pure invention of the orator, and that no such person had ever existed, so that they laughed "consumedly." They were wrong, C. V. B. (excuse the abbreviation) was no myth, but the author of ponderous but clever quarto volumes on International Law. By the way, it is difficult to account for the strange fact, that three out of the four authorities that carry such weight on so important a subject, were natives or denizens of Holland. What is the secret of this peculiar aptitude of Dutchmen for the Jus Gentium ?

interval of peace (for the din of war drowns the voice of reason) would ensure its success.

3rd. A clear definition of the duties devolving on, and an equally clear limitation of the powers entrusted to, our ambassadors to foreign states, would greatly conduce to the interests of peace. It is demonstrable from history that these personages have, if not caused, at least fomented many wars that might not have taken place but for their well-meant but unfortunate activity. They are often placed in such a position that they must either be mischievous or inactive. Their path to distinction lies in the display of zeal and energy, and these are precisely the qualities which, in the majority of cases, tend to entangle us in political controversies. A stolid inertness, a love for the "*dolce far niente*," a quiet indifference—these are the modest endowments which we should most covet in our representatives abroad. As Talleyrand said to a newly-fledged diplomatist, "*Et surtout, point de zèle.*" Unfortunately these negative virtues do not lead to celebrity, and never lift the slow, but innocuous functionary into the highest post in Downing Street.

Happy the nation whose ambassadors are not men of genius! The restless activity of such aspiring intellects swells the importance of every topic, and fills each channel of communication to overflowing. They advise their governments of everything, great or small, that passes in the state to which they are accredited. Nothing escapes them. Every change, either in the official hierarchy or in the objects of personal favouritism ; every tendency, real or supposed, towards a fluctuation of policy ; every private circumstance affecting persons in office ; every symptom of internal weakness ; and all sorts of rumours, scandals, and trivialities, form the staple of either official or confidential reports, on which the issues of war or peace often depend. From such advices, copious yet incomplete, apparently impartial, yet unwittingly deceptive, national misunderstandings have frequently arisen.

Moreover, it sometimes happens that a zealous ambassador to a country torn by internal dissensions, conceives it his duty to entertain special relations with the strongest party ; but, misled by some clique or coterie, he makes an erroneous selection, and finds that he has linked his government with a losing minority. Hence heart-burnings and feuds between nations who, but for diplomacy, would have been on terms, not indeed of dangerous intimacy, but of permanent friendly intercourse.

CHAPTER XXI.

Fifth argument in favour of a policy of isolation.

OUR EXAMPLE MAY INDUCE OTHER STATES TO ADOPT
A SIMILAR POLICY.

THE subject of international policy has been
treated in these pages principally with reference
to the well-being of England, to which country
some of the arguments adduced more especially
apply. But the general principles advocated are
true in regard to all nations ; for if each confined
its attention to the promotion of its own welfare,
all would feel the benefit of that course in the
uninterrupted development of their resources.
In proportion to the concentration of each state
within itself, would the existing causes for collision with its neighbours be eliminated, and the
chances of permanent peace be multiplied.

To this happy result nothing would more
powerfully conduce than our successful initiation
of the policy. It must be borne in mind that
those countries which are conterminous have
greater difficulties to contend with than we have.
They are more exposed to attack. With us,
there is a sea to traverse. With them there
may be a river to cross, a mountain range to
scale, or a few frontier-fortresses either to

capture or to elude ; but, war once declared,
the deadly struggle is speedily imminent, if not
immediate.

Moreover, border districts are generally of
ill-defined nationality. The line between the
inhabitants of Dover and those of Calais is
sharply drawn. Their language, religion, habits,
tastes, dress, &c., are as strikingly contrasted as
though their habitations were five hundred miles
apart. But where France touches Germany,
Italy, or Spain, or where Germany abuts on
Switzerland, Denmark, or the Netherlands, a
certain degree of imperfect fusion occurs. The
inhabitants of frontier regions are mostly a
mixed race. They either speak a dialect
peculiar to themselves, or use, with idiomatic
modifications, the languages of both the countries
which they fringe. Their habits are of a hybrid
character, and their political predilections lean
sometimes to one side, sometimes to the other.
The equivocal position of these unfortunate
districts has made them a bone of contention
between powerful states. From this cause their
soil is dotted over with celebrated battle-fields,
and they have from time to time changed mas-
ters, as the fortune of war, *nunc mihi, nunc aliis
benigna*, may have decided. The close promixity
of contiguous countries on the one hand, and the

periodical changes in their boundaries on the
other, present some impediments to the adoption
of a policy of isolation from which we are free.
Hence it is the more incumbent on us to set the
example, since we are exempt from the dangers
arising from the former predicament, and from
the temptations presented by the latter. Our
adoption of such a policy would be regarded as
an important experiment, the results of which
would be closely scanned by the world, whilst
its success would lead our neighbours gradually,
but irresistibly, into the same career of improvement.

———•———.

CHAPTER XXII.

*Europe not a confederation of states. Tendency of com-
munities to consolidate into lingual groups.*

IF Europe really formed a confederation of
states, bound together by regulations which en-
sured the peaceable submission of the minority
to the decrees of the majority, the objections to
our joint liability with them would even then
not be removed, though somewhat weakened. It
is most probable that such a combination would
work no better than its Grecian prototype, the
Amphictyonic council, but it would present a

certain symmetry of design far more likely to produce good results than the present chaotic practice of one, two, or three states interfering at fitful intervals and with fitful energy with the concerns of one, two, or three other states.

But Europe is not a confederation of states, and all arguments in favour of the intervention-system founded on such an assumption are illusory. Most European states (or rather their governments) aspire to a *status*, and entertain designs, altogether incompatible with the aspirations and designs of their neighbours ; and with adverse, not common interests, federation is impossible.

Had the theory of " upholding the balance of power " been recognized and successfully adopted some five hundred years ago, Europe would now have been composed of more than a hundred independent and discordant governments. In Italy, for instance, every large town was then a state. These in course of time clustered into duchies, principalities, and small kingdoms, and it is but recently that they have merged into one powerful nation. Germany, at the period referred to, consisted of an infinite number of independent electorates, dukedoms, bishoprics, free towns, &c., which have only just been fused into one mighty empire. Had the mania for the "balance of power" prevailed at that period, and its doctrines been enforced by physical force, there would have been no great French nation. Guyenne would have remained an English possession, and the Dukes of Burgundy would still have reigned over several of the fairest provinces of France. The stream of events flows onwards in spite of the petty obstacles of political manœuvres.

There appears to be a normal tendency to the absorption of small by large states, just as rills combine to form rivers, which are themselves destined to be engulphed in the vast ocean. But there is a specific limit to this consodidation of states, which has its origin in dissimilarity of language, religion, and habits. Where this unconformity exists, fusion is difficult in spite of physical force. Where it does not exist, the tendency to fusion cannot be suppressed by political combinations.

Identity of language is a fair exponent of the tendency to amalgamation. It mostly implies identity of race, and occasionally the complete incorporation of one nationality into another. With few exceptions, it implies identity of religion and similarity of habits. These form the essential elements of thorough fusion. From these arises the tendency towards the agglomera-

tion into one state of the populations which speak
the same language. On the other hand, the
compulsory cohesion of races, whose language and
literature have nothing in common, can be but
temporary, even when enforced at the point of
the bayonet, and they will assuredly fall asunder
when the pressure is removed. As a notable
instance of the futility of mere statecraft in
opposition to national antipathies, may be quoted
the attempted amalgamation of Holland and
Belgium at the bidding of the omnipotent congress of 1814. This marriage "by command"
of two nations, whose language and religion
utterly differed, and whose mutual dislike to the
"match" was scornfully disregarded by its
powerful promoters (chiefly England), led, like
many other *mariages de convenance*, to domestic
dissensions, and finally, after sixteen years of
discord and strife, to a complete divorce in 1830.
In that year Belgium revolted from the Dutch
yoke, and of that revolt an able representative
of the old English policy speaks in the following
terms (Sir H. Bulwer's "Life of Lord Palmerston," Vol. II. p. 2). " The insurrection by which
we were (in 1830) most affected was the Belgian
one. We had sufficiently learnt the danger and
the cost of having to watch and defend ourselves
against an enemy possessing the long line of

coast by which we had been hostilely confronted during the reign of Napoleon. . . . . We had imagined that we had avoided this danger by uniting Holland with Belgium, hoping thus to have created a powerful kingdom, of which we had protected the frontier by fortresses raised under our inspection and in some degree at our expense."

Here we may incidentally note that this compulsory junction of the Dutch and Belgian people was enforced, not for their benefit, not with their concurrence, not indeed, with any reference to their interests or wishes, but solely in compliance with the desire of England to artificially "create a powerful kingdom," in whose custody Antwerp and the adjacent line of coast should be secure from French occupancy.

But this cunning fabric crumbled into dust within a few years. Belgium achieved her independence, and became the free and prosperous country which we see her now. But to keep up the "policy," and in substitution for the "powerful kingdom," the formation of which the scission between Belgium and Holland had rendered impossible, we entered into fresh complications, and combined with other states to guarantee the neutrality of Belgium, so as still to keep the French from Antwerp.

By this course we entered into a bond to go

to war, 1st. Whenever Belgium should choose to take part in any continental struggle ; 2nd. Whenever any state should, rightly or wrongly, declare war against Belgium ; 3rd. Whenever Belgium should be convicted of violating the laws of neutrality in time of war, and therefore exposed to attack from one of the belligerents ; 4th. Whenever Belgium should sympathise with a cause to which we were hostile ; 5th. Whenever Belgium should spontaneously think fit to merge her separate existence, and incorporate herself with another nation. In short, whenever any circumstance occurred to alter the relations subsisting between Belgium and any other country. Thus did we thickly sow the seeds of future wars.

CHAPTER XXIII.

Influence of war on the interests of wage-receivers.

THE receivers of wages in payment for labour are usually denominated the working-class, but improperly, as this classification embraces two divisions essentially distinct. It is not that wage-receivers are not workers, and hard enough workers, too, but that others who are not wage-

receivers are also workers in the widest sense of
the term. The member of parliament and the
statesman, the merchant and the manufacturer,
the physician and the lawyer, the author and
the artist, the tradesman and the farmer, labour
as hard, either with the brain or with the hand,
as any artisan or journeyman, and come as
correctly under the designation of working-class.
But they are payers, not receivers of wages ;
and those who use the term "working-class"
have the latter only in view, and totally exclude
the former. A denomination, therefore, which
includes them both is illogical and misleading,
and should not be used when the intention is to
refer to one only.

The payers of wages consist, with very few
exceptions,—

1st. Of those who have themselves amassed
savings by spending less than they earned.

2nd. Of those who have inherited the savings
of others, mostly acquired by the same process
of spending less than they earned.

The receivers of wages consist of those who,
either from not earning enough or from spending
too much, have not accumulated any savings,
and sell their labour to those who have saved.
But whenever a wage-receiver has, either by
hard work or frugality, laid by a sum of money

or a store of goods, he becomes to that extent
a savings-holder, or in other terms a capitalist.
Capital is composed of accumulated savings,
and all savings are capital, whether the amount
be large or small.

Wage-receivers complain that the productions,
to which their labour has contributed at least as
much as the capital of the savings-holder, are
unequally distributed, and that the latter gets
the lion's share. Into this question the scope
of this work precludes us from entering ; but
this much is certain, viz. : that everything which
checks and diminishes production is peculiarly
injurious to the wage-receiver. There is nothing
produced that is not ultimately distributed,
except what is consumed by fire or lost by ship-
wreck, or wasted, where produced, from difficulties
of transit. The larger the store of those things
which minister to the necessities and comforts
of men, the greater the share that must fall to
each. Even admitting inequality of distribution,
it is evident that all recipients, large or small,
are benefited more or less by the greater abun-
dance of the things distributed.

To stop production imports privation for a
certain number of human beings. To the
savings-holder (or capitalist) it merely implies
some encroachment upon his savings ; but to

the wage-receiver it implies a diminished demand for his only commodity, labour, and consequently penury and distress.

Whatever tends to enlarge the stock of necessaries and comforts distributable amongst the human family is a benefit and a blessing. Whatever tends to contract it is a scourge and a crime, from which all suffer, and it is on the poor that the suffering weighs most heavily.

There are many human agencies, all evil and all remediable, which in the fatal manner described interfere with production ; but none of them is at once so baneful and so inexcusable as war.*

It removes men in the prime of life from their

---

* A long catalogue might easily be drawn up of the pernicious influences which, as well as war, though in minor degree, interfere with productive operations.   Some of the most obvious of them may be here enumerated, viz. :—

1st. National debts.

2nd. Prohibitory or protective duties.

3rd. Laws tending to keep large tracts of land out of cultivation.

4th. Redundance in the number of, and in the payments to, public functionaries.

5th. Insecurity of life and property deterring savings-holders from investment.

6th. Ignorance.

7th. Pauperism.

8th. Unduly depressed rates of wages.

9th. Trades unions as far as, by strikes, &c., they obstruct production.

Cum multis aliis.

natural position as bread-winners, and turns them into unproductive and destructive consumers. It kills or maims a part of them, and those the bravest and the manliest. It squanders talent and labour on the invention and manufacture of murderous implements. It lays fields waste, and converts towns and villages into mounds of rubbish. It inflicts a heavy weight of taxation upon the people, to be borne even unto remote generations. In short, in a hundred different ways, it at once dissipates the fund from which provision is made for the wants of the community by wasting previous accumulations, and prevents its replenishment by arresting production.

True, that the lottery of war sometimes affords, amidst its millions of blanks, a few prizes ; but to whom do they fall ? Very seldom to the privates.

To the wage receivers, therefore, war, being exceptionally pernicious, should be specially hateful, and it behoves them to support a policy which would reduce to a *minimum* the chances of a calamity so peculiarly fatal to their interests.

CHAPTER XXIV.

Movement of political power, and intellectual energy, from East to West.

OUR exaggerated attention to European politics is partly attributable to habit and routine. For some ages past, Europe has been the centre of civilization, and has wielded the sceptre of political and military supremacy. We have accustomed ourselves to consider this the normal state of Europe's relation to the rest of the world. But this small quarter of the globe has not always occupied that high position, and if we are to judge of the future course of political changes by the operation of a certain constant law that has regulated their vicissitudes since the earliest period of historical records, that pre-eminence will probably not be enduring.

If we review the successive rise and fall of the ruling empires of the world from the time that the transactions of the human race were first chronicled, we shall observe that the movement of political power has uniformly been from the east to the west.

Of all national records, none claim so remote an antiquity for the people of whom they profess to be the annals as those of China, at the extreme east of Asia, and those of Hindoostan, one step forward in the westerly direction. Then, after a certain interval, followed an epoch during which the more western regions of Asia obtained the chief prominence, and became the seat of the leading nations of the world. The glories of Nineveh and ·Babylon stood unrivalled in their age, and the sculptured trophies of their numerous conquests may be seen in our museums even unto the present day. Old Egypt, their contemporary, and sometimes their rival, reigned supreme in the extreme north-east corner of Africa, and bequeathed to after ages those stupendous monuments which still give a kind of dead life to her sandy plains.

Europe, meanwhile, was one vast forest, tenanted by a few savages. But at last, kindling at the flame which still rolled onward from the east, Greece succeeded to the sceptre of power, civilization, and art. For two centuries Greece produced a far greater number of statesmen, legists, warriors, orators, philosophers, poets, historians, painters, sculptors, architects, &c., than any other nation, with tenfold the population, has in any age produced within the same space of time. Finally trampled on by Macedon, and soon subsiding into a Roman province, Greece lost her pre-eminence, and the empire of

I

the world, still travelling westward, was transferred to Rome, which, after crushing Carthage, became the foremost of nations.

Then occurred an interregnum, during which the torch of civilization was all but quenched, and finally an amalgamation took place between Rome and her barbaric invaders, resulting, after centuries of darkness, in the present form of European polity and civilization. Spain, Germany, France, and England, acquired great political importance. Learning and science revived, and the most important fruit of this renewed intellectual movement was, after the invention of printing, the discovery of America by Columbus.

It was at the precise moment when further progress westward appeared to have reached its utmost limit on the shores of western Europe, that the new world, still further to the west, loomed in sight to afford an opportunity for advance, in the same old direction, of social organization and political power.

Spain first, ineffectually by conquest, and England afterwards, effectually by colonization, ferried civilization across the Atlantic. The eastern seaboard of America became the seat of a civilized, energetic, and rapidly expanding offshoot from the old Anglo-Saxon race. The same indomitable spirit of enterprize which carried the Vikings of our ancestors westward across the seas, to fresh pastures and new homes, led the hardy back-settlers of the American republic, still westward, on to the fertile valleys of the Ohio and the Mississippi.

Scarcely were these vast alluvial plains scantily populated when the restless spirit of migration lured the colonist across the rocky mountains and the vast desert of which the great Salt Lake is at once the centre and the representative, still westward, and lodged him in the teeming fields, auriferous gullies, and matchless climate of California and Oregon.

At this point, further progress westward is arrested by the North Pacific Ocean, which bathes the shores, both of California ,to which the latest scintillations of civilization have penetrated, and of China, whence the oldest extant written traditions affirm the first glimmerings of civilization to have radiated eastward. Thus, after long ages, is the cycle complete, and the old and almost fossilized civilization of China is linked with the new and rapidly developing civilization of San Francisco.

Curiously enough, it would appear, by the increasing emigration of the Chinese into California, and the disinclination of the Americans

to push further westward into China, as if the
westward tide, having reached its limit, were
exhibiting symptoms of reversal; and as if
China, having formerly been the starting point
westward, were now likely to become the starting
point eastward. This, however, is a speculation
most diffidently advanced, since it rests on only
one or two data ; but the movement from east
to west has, for a long series of ages, glided
almost uninterruptedly in that direction. During
this gradual transference westward of political power and intellectual energy, there have
occurred several waves of temporary or apparent
opposition to the general current (like eddies
from minor obstacles in a rapid river), but, in the
main, the stream has flowed with persistent
constancy.

It is not intended to assert that the cycle is
complete in every sense. Europe has not become as effete as had Asia when Europe obtained
its undisputed ascendancy. Nor has America
as yet achieved that supremacy over Europe
that Europe achieved over Asia. But it is wave
by wave, and not at one swoop, that the tide
rises and makes the dry beach a prey to the
waters ; and the impulse that has converted the
wilds of north western America into cornfields,
—that has peopled them with rapidly increasing

cities,—and is gradually netting them with rail-ways, has by no means reached its full *momentum*. The prosperity of nations is seldom stationary. Continental Europe must either advance or retrograde. To its advance, so as to keep pace with western progress, there are many obstacles. Of these, not the least formidable are—1st, its addiction to internecine wars; and 2nd, its neglect of the immense world outside of it for the petty interests within its contracted circle. To these causes its ultimate decadence, should it occur, will be largely owing.

It is for us, whose blood flows in the veins of 80,000,000 of people who are now converting millions of square miles in America, Australia, the Cape, and elsewhere, from haunts for wild beasts into homes and habitations for men, to inquire seriously with which race we are to cast in our future lot. With the strangers—the Celts, the Latins, the Sclavonians, and the Turks of old Europe, or with our own kith and kin, the energetic and progressive Anglo-Saxons of the wide world? With the stagnant, or with the growing races? With the failing past, or with the budding future?

CHAPTER XXV.

Vast increase presumable in the population of the globe, and as to the races of which this increase will be mostly composed. Probable preponderance of the Anglo-Saxon race.

WERE Europe the only quarter of the globe in which modern civilization could flourish, the future destinies of the human race would have to be considered in reference to that region alone, and the expansion of human progress would be circumscribed within its limited area. But Europe forms but a fractional part of the habitable globe. Vast tracts of land, equal in extent to many Europes, are waiting to be converted by civilized man, from weed-producing wildernesses, into fertile fields teeming with wealth. The work has already commenced on a small scale, and a scanty portion of those dreary wastes, the future abode of mighty nations, has been occupied and cultivated. By far the greatest portion, however, still remains to be redeemed from inutility by the agency of human labour.

In prosperous countries, the births exceed the deaths in such a ratio as, after a time, to cause the land to overflow with population. The

annual percentage of increase may vary, but it
is only in feeble or decadent nations that the
population is stagnant or retrograde. Whither
is that prolificness leading us? Is the world
destined to realize the Malthusian difficulty?
Be this as it may, we are, at all events, not
bound at present to provide against an evil
which is purely theoretical, and which, at any
rate, cannot press heavily until that distant
period arrives when all the habitable zones of
the earth are converted into a garden. To
thwart nature, crush our instincts, and create
immediate misery in order to avoid a suppo-
sititious and confessedly remote danger would
be absurd. "Sufficient for the day is the evil
thereof." Cobbett, a rough, shrewd thinker,
contended, in opposition to Malthus, that as
long as men were born with two arms to work
with, mother earth would supply their wants.

How long a time must elapse before the world
could possibly be saturated with people, may be
conjectured from the following calculation :—
The area of the Brazilian Empire is 3,100,104
square miles. Supposing it to become as densely
populated as is Belgium at the present day (432
persons per square mile), that country alone
could accommodate upwards of 1,300,000,000
of human beings, whilst the actual population

of the entire globe is estimated at about 1,000,000,000. At present, the population of the Brazils is about 10,000,000.

It is true, that in taking Belgium as a standard, we have selected the country that can boast the densest population in the world. But there is no reason why other countries should not reach or even exceed that standard. We observe no symptoms of Belgium having attained her maximum density. There exists no pressure on her resources; she is remarkably free from pauperism, and the proportion of wage-payers, as compared with wage-receivers, is exceptionally large. This prosperity, actual and prospective, is no doubt owing to the intelligence, industry, and thrift of the Belgian people, and to the excellence of their government; but there is no reason why, in other countries, similar causes should not produce similar effects.

The population of China averages about 300 human beings per square mile, but it is very unequally distributed. In some provinces it is sparse, in others it is crowded to redundancy. But, taking China as a whole, if those regions of the earth that possess the same capabilities for ministering to man's wants were to be cultivated with the same industry, it would be difficult to assign a limit to the possible multiplication of mankind.

The population of Great Britain and Ireland cannot, by this time, fall far short in density from that of China. But there is plenty of room for further increase. Large tracts of land throughout the United Kingdom are lying as useless as the prairies of America, whilst, at the same time, we yearly expatriate thousands of families, thousands of miles away, to expend their labour on soils whose produce may be more abundant, but the remoteness of which from a high-priced market renders less valuable. Were that area which is now artificially and unnecessarily withdrawn from tillage brought into cultivation, England could support a large addition to her present occupants.*

* That the laws affecting the tenure of land imperatively call for revision, is now pretty generally admitted. From the peculiar enactments affecting the distribution and sale of land, large masses of it have come to be tabood from the use of man. Many thousands of these useless acres have, by some ancient and mystical feudal process, fallen under the control of a number of persons called copyholders, headed by the possessor of some undefined rights called the lord of the manor. These co-owners generally disagree as to the disposal of the property, so that it is condemned to sterility, and left to the geese and donkeys, who alone derive some infinitesimally small benefit from it. Other large areas of land are owned by many-acred paupers, who have not the means, or in some cases have not the brains, to improve their possessions, and yet will not sell them to others who have both. Sometimes settlements and entails tie up land in so

From what precedes and from other estimates carefully framed, it is presumable that after every deduction has been made for those large portions of the globe which, from extreme cold and extreme heat, are unavailable as residences for man,—as also for deserts, mountain ranges, and other uncultivable spots, the present population of the globe might easily be multiplied fourfold. In other words, the earth is capable of maintaining at least 3000 millions of people,

---

intricate a knot that force alone, not patience, will be adequate to its disentanglement. In several other ways, too, land is absorbed for totally unproductive purposes ; and the earth, in which all human beings have a common birthright, and which has only been divided into proprietorships by either brute force or conventional arrangements, is partially diverted from its legitimate function and designedly devoted to barrenness. This state of things cannot endure indefinitely, and the extent of individual rights to neutralize the bounty of nature will, sooner or later, become a subject for Parliament to examine and define. A capitalist who should dig a hole and bury in it a million of sovereigns, would not by his act sensibly influence the well-being of his countrymen ; but if three or four wealthy men were to club together and buy up Lincolnshire, evict the farmers and the other tenants, and do with it what William the Conqueror did with the New Forest, all England would rise up against it. And yet it would be perfectly legal. Not one tittle of either common or statute law need be violated. It would simply be a case of "*Summum jus, summa injuria.*" To what extent land is a different kind of commodity from all others, partly through being limited to a certain absolute quantity, and partly through its exceptional peculiarity of not being conveyable from place to place, is an enquiry which would lead us into far too aberrant a disquisition.

in addition to those by which it is at present tenanted.

It does not appear that, for ages past, there has been any very sensible increase in the aggregate population of the globe. For a long while it stood at an estimate of 1000 millions ; and the latest inquirers assess it variously at from 950 to 1350 millions. But this comparative stagnation is not likely to continue under the kindling influences of steam, which neutralizes distance, and telegraphy, which condenses time. The tide of humanity is rapidly flooding beyond its old boundaries, and the vast gap that exists between the actual and the possible population of the earth is likely henceforth to be rapidly filled up.

Of what race or races the enormous multitudes who will then overspread the habitable parts of the globe will be mainly composed, can only be a matter of conjecture. But if we are to be guided by analogy, the task of replenishing the earth will devolve on those families of men that possess the greatest vitality, energy, and prolificness. If so, the contest will probably be between the old Chinese (or Mongolian) family, and the modern Anglo-Saxon tribes.*

* It is a curious and suggestive fact, that both these great divisions of the human race are, in contrast to the rest of the world, tea drinkers.

The Chinese and their congeners, at present, constitute about one-third of the human race, and, in olden times, must have formed a still larger proportion. Their peculiar laws have for centuries isolated them from the rest of mankind, and, by compressing the race within certain territorial limits, have counteracted its expansibility. Should that people, however, as seems probable, level these artificial barriers, and send their redundant population forth to occupy other lands, the progress of this industrious, frugal, and prolific race, would reassume the rapid flow which governmental repression had arrested.

But it is to the Anglo-Saxon race that we must look as likely to contribute by far the largest contingent to the vast host by which the habitable globe will eventually be overspread and populated.* The fecundity and consequent rapid increase, the energy and consequent restless spirit of enterprise of this race are without precedent in the past, and without parallel in the present. The first English settlers in North

---

* It is as well to explain that throughout this work the expression, "Anglo-Saxons," is intended to embrace all the English-speaking populations. In a strictly ethnological sense the definition may be liable to exceptions, but with this explanation it clearly conveys the meaning of the writer, as the lingual test is precise and unmistakable.

America,—the handful of men who inaugurated a system of colonization destined to produce gigantic results, radiated from a small and thinly populated country, barely numbering 6,000,000 of inhabitants. To-day, the metropolis of the old mother-country alone contains half that number, and is the largest city in the world. A census now taken of the English-speaking people, scattered throughout the world in larger or smaller masses, would give a return nearly approaching to 80,000,000. Two generations hence, it is presumable that this number may swell to 200,000,000, and it will still continue to expand in a rapid ratio. Nothing indicates any relaxation in the colonizing energy of our race. Our American and Australian brethren are pushing their bloodless conquests over willing nature with unabated vigour. Primeval forests and trackless prairies are being invaded by railroads and telegraph wires, and will in time be wholly, as they are now to a small extent, enrolled in the service of man. It is under circumstances akin to these that, as experience has shown, the human species reproduces and multiplies itself with the greatest rapidity.

We find that the Anglo-Saxon race has increased thirteenfold in 250 years. Were this rate of increase to be sustained, there is nothing

but what is reasonable in the expectation that
the 3000 millions of human beings still wanting to complete the world's population may
be supplied at no very remote period of time.
At all events, a mighty accession will accrue
from generation to generation, and unless other
nations exhibit corresponding expansion, this
increment will be recruited principally from the
Anglo-Saxon race.

In continental Europe, two races alone have
exhibited any marked tendency to expansion,
viz., the Sclavonian and Teutonic. The others
have increased but slowly, and some, such as
France, Spain, Turkey, &c., are almost stagnant;
moreover, none of these show any aptitude for
colonization.

The Sclavonic races form a vast body numbering about 75,000,000 of people, but their rate
of increase is slow, and they still have enormous
tracts of land of their own to fill before they
spread into distant climes. These two considerations render it unlikely that they will for
many ages contribute much towards populating
the other unfilled spaces of the earth.

The Germans multiply faster, and, next to the
Anglo-Saxons, show the greatest aptitude for
colonization. Besides forming some few settlements in Russia, they have emigrated largely to

the United States of America, where they have grouped themselves into communities, in which the German language and German habits more or less prevail. But this isolation proves but temporary. They are too few in number to resist the disintegrating influences of the masses around them; and they are finally assimilated and absorbed by the Anglo-Saxon people amongst whom they have cast their lot. This process of fusion must always take place, sooner or later, when a small body effects a junction with a large one, just as a river, however mighty, loses its identity when it merges into the ocean.

The remarks which precede, as to the probable future population of the earth, have an important bearing on the views propounded in these pages as to our foreign policy. If the tendency of events is to leave Europe stationary in the face of mighty nations swiftly growing into unapproachable preponderance, it is surely a vital question how far and in what direction these vast impending changes are to influence our future policy. Are we still to link our destinies with those of continental Europe, or are we to break away from the entanglement and cohere with the great and growing Anglo-Saxon system?

Europe consists of a cluster of small, infusible,

discordant, and inelastic states, of which it has become the fixed habit to subordinate peace and commerce to selfish aggrandizement and the lurid glare of military glory.

On the other hand lies the wide world, soon to be overspread by mighty nations more populous and wealthy; infinitely more energetic and progressive, and, at the same time, more peaceful and law-abiding.

There can be no hesitation as to the choice.

The shadows which coming events cast before them afford to the statesman safe landmarks by which to steer his course, just as a distant object visible to the traveller enables him to push straight to his destination; whilst both are liable to lose their way, if they confine their examination to their immediate surroundings. The future, when viewed in its true colossal dimensions, dwarfs the present into comparative insignificance. As the human race multiplies, and new communities are formed, the distribution of political power undergoes corresponding modification. We are the seminal people from which those nations will have sprung which are probably to be the future arbiters of the world's destiny. Happy for us if we grow with them, coalesce with them, identify ourselves with them, and become part of the great cosmic system from which alone we can hope for that progress towards man's social well-being which the old civilization of Europe has so wofully failed in securing.

Man is, if not a perfectible, at least an improvable being; but his progress is miserably incomplete if it is limited to the development of his physical and intellectual faculties. His only true aim is happiness, to attain which the moral and spiritual part of his nature also requires adequate development. It is possible for a man to be ignorant, and yet conscientious and virtuous according to his lights, and therefore happy. But a man may possess the intellect and acquirements of a Newton, and yet he will feel his life a burthen if he be the slave of his animal passions, and stifle those moral instincts which, collectively, are called conscience. So it is with nations. It is possible for a community to be poor and yet contented and happy. But a country may be as powerful as France under the first Napoleon, or as Spain under the second Philip; it may enrol its victories on monuments of bronze and marble; and yet the mass of its inhabitants may be individually wretched and discontented.

The Anglo-Saxon race have always displayed a peculiar appreciation of this distinction, and have assiduously cultivated the arts of peace.

K

Amidst all the turmoils of political strife, in-
industrial and commercial pursuits have, amongst
them, met with due attention. Nor has this
circumstance rendered the race inapt for war.
Quite the contrary : in many a hard-fought
contest, from Cressy to Inkermann, from the
Armada to Trafalgar, from Bunker's Hill to
Richmond, they have proved how well they
could fight when that melancholy duty was
assigned to them. But the triumphs of agriculture, manufactures, and commerce—triumphs
the more glorious because, in these, all are
crowned, and none are victims—are still more
prized by our people.

We are called a nation of shop-keepers, and
our American brethren are taxed with philo-
dollarism ; but these expressions are simply a
caricature. They are intended to typify, in an
exaggerated form, the legitimate pursuits of
honest industry in contradistinction to rapine
and cut-throatism. So Falstaff, when robbing
the travellers, calls them "fat chuffs" and "gor-
bellied knaves ;" so the brigands of Calabria and
the Klephts of Greece affect contempt for the
burghers whom they capture and rob ; so the
Huns and Vandals treated with contumelious
derision the peaceful citizens of the towns which
they demolished. But there is no logical signi-

ficance in the taunt. Those institutions which, by fostering industry and commerce, promote the "greatest happiness of the greatest number," are beneficent and ennobling. Those which pander to the evil passions of men, and foment lust of dominion and brutal thirst for war, are wicked and debasing. Call these by what name you will, the facts will still remain the same.

Wherever they may have settled—north, south, east, or west—let us stand by our own people,— our kith and kin,—the issue of our loins,—whose blood is our blood,—who think, speak, and write in one common language,—whose mental pulse vibrates with our own,—who drink at the same intellectual fount,—who have the same tastes and aspirations, and perhaps the same failings and demerits as ourselves. Their sympathies are still with the old mother-country, England, as ours ought to be with them. A jarring note may occasionally have disturbed the harmony of our intercourse, but there is no family, however united, that can be totally free from such dissonance ; and when hushed, there generally succeeds more perfect concord and more intimate union.

We believe, as well as hope, that a day will come when the several English-speaking coun- tries will organize a great Anglo-Saxon confederation. It will not be intended to encroach on the autonomy or independence of each state, but it will have for object to settle all questions or differences that may arise between them by a council, in which each will be represented, and of which the decisions by a majority of votes will be final. Amongst us Anglo-Saxons, it is an understood and habitual practice to allow the majority to govern. The minority may be unconvinced, but it submits. It may endeavour by discussion, argument, or persuasion to acquire a numerical superiority, but till then, it accepts its position and obeys the law. This acknowledgment of the supremacy of the majority lies at the base of all republican institutions, and where it is contravened and the minority assumes the right of physical resistance, a commonwealth is impossible. Civil strife then becomes the normal condition of the community, and the only cure lies in the other desperate extreme, a despotism. All republican institutions (whether the chief magistrate be hereditary or elective) exist under the inevitable condition that the minority will gracefully bow to the decisions of the majority. The impulsive Celts and Latins cannot understand this, but the Anglo-Saxons have, for many generations, acted on that principle. Hence it is that we derive the hope that a solution to all international difficulties, and the solid establishment of perennial peace, would be the blessed result of a great federation of all those English-speaking populations by which, according to all human probability, the largest portion of the habitable globe will be eventually overspread.

THE END.

LONDON : EDWARD STANFORD, 6 AND 7 CHARING CROSS.

www.ingramcontent.com/pod-product-compliance
Lightning Source LLC
Chambersburg PA
CBHW030608270326
41927CB00007B/1094